Practical Jaguar Ownership

A word of warning to wives: Don't bank on a lift to the shops if he says "Won't be long – just got a couple of things to do on the Jag..."

Practical Jaguar Ownership

How to extend the life of a well-worn 'cat'

MARTIN CROSS
Drawings by ALAN MARSH

MRP

MOTOR RACING PUBLICATIONS LTD
Unit 6, The Pilton Estate, 46 Pitlake, Croydon CR0 3RY, England

First published 1997

British Library Cataloguing in Publication Data

Cross, Martin
  Practical Jaguar ownership : how to extend the life of a
  well-worn 'cat'
  1. Jaguar automobile 2. Jaguar automobile – Conservation and
  restoration
  I. Title
  629.2'222

ISBN 1-899870-24-5

Typeset by JDB Typesetting
Printed in Great Britain by The Amadeus Press Ltd, Huddersfield, England

Contents

SS 100. One careful owner. Only used for country touring and regularly washed.

Introduction

With so many well-written and informative books about Jaguars already on the market, is there a need for yet another? Well, I for one like to think so, not because I am able to reveal any previously unpublished facts about the company's history, or about the innermost workings of the cars it produced, but because I am probably one of those people whom William Lyons most had in mind when he launched the Jaguar marque all those years ago. Yes, I am one of those who, having cast my eyes on a Jaguar for the first time, instantly became hooked and, despite all the tribulations that have accompanied subsequent ownership, have been prepared to forgive the shortcomings, learn from the experience, and willingly come back for more.

I became a Jaguar 'nut' a long time ago, and because we are a far from dying breed – indeed I believe our species has never been less vulnerable to extinction than today – I like to think that there are many of you out there who might like to know about, and perhaps through this book benefit from, the practical knowledge that I have accumulated over many years of owning, running and maintaining a huge variety of models as well as helping to refurbish many more which have been owned by others.

This book, therefore, is a first-hand account of a life spent in, around, and quite often underneath Jaguars of all sizes, shapes and ages, enjoying a very special type of relationship with cars of unique character, whose strengths are such that they tend to overwhelm their readily identifiable weaknesses. It is, in other words, a book by a Jaguar enthusiast aimed specifically at fellow enthusiasts – past, present and, hopefully, future.

I emphasise future because one of my prime aims is to convince the doubters that ownership of a well-worn Jaguar is not necessarily a passport to certain financial ruin, far from it, in fact. I hope I shall be able to demonstrate that, tackled sensibly, putting a Jaguar in the garage or on the driveway can be a surprisingly economical form of pleasurable motoring, especially for those of a practical nature who are not afraid to get their hands dirty in pursuit of making something very appealing even more so.

As much of what you will read in this book will be concerned with refurbishing and improving the car, I should explain right away that I have not been, nor am I ever likely to be, part of the so-called classic car scene, in which I have no interest whatsoever. Most of the 25 or so SS and Jaguar cars which have passed through my hands have been older models (the earliest was built in 1936), which to many people these days seems to imply that they are automatically 'classics'. I'm sorry, but I cannot see how a car can earn such an accolade simply because of its age, nor do I gain any pleasure in seeing an older Jaguar so over-restored in pursuit of *concours d'elegance* fame that its owner is constantly looking skywards, petrified that a drop of rain will fall upon the outermost of the 15 coats of paint applied to its gleaming bodywork.

I like to think that I have refurbished many cars to a high standard, but I have never knowingly been guilty of over-restoration; in my opinion the ultimate effect when the job is complete should correspond to the sort of appearance one might expect from a carefully maintained car which has been on the road for a year or so. I never lose sight of the fact that cars were built to be used, not to be ferried around the countryside on trailers and paraded in front of scrutineers. What I shall be writing about, therefore, is likely to win you no prizes at your next classic car competition. But if, like me, you believe that the joy of owning a Jaguar is to enjoy driving it on every possible occasion, I hope you will find on these pages some useful guidance towards prolonging your car's usefulness and perhaps improving its appearance and comfort. I also hope that I make a convincing case for being a Jaguar 'nut'!

Stockport, Cheshire
1997

MARTIN CROSS

Acknowledgements

When I set out to write this book, I had little idea of the magnitude of the task I had undertaken. But the project would have been even more time-consuming, and the end product much the poorer, but for the help that was so generously provided for me from friends and fellow Jaguar enthusiasts.

In particular I would like to thank John Sundberg, of A&B Leather Renovations, who gave me the benefit of his consumate skill and advice in preparing the chapter on interior restoration, as well as providing a selection of photographs with which to illustrate it. I also owe a double debt of gratitude to Ian Cooling, for not only was much of the information contained in the final chapter drawn from features in his excellent magazine *Jaguar Automobilia Collector*, but he then painstakingly checked my manuscript and added valuable new data which had been revealed through his never-ending researches. He and Michael Tate, who contributes to Ian's magazine, supplied photographs for this chapter, while I am indebted to Michael Thurston, who provided the print of his magnificent display of Jaguar badges.

Several of my Jaguar-owning friends burst into print with their recollections, which I have been pleased to include, and I am most grateful to them all for jogging their memories. Finally, I must record my sincere thanks to that talented artist Alan Marsh who, although we have never met, has managed through his drawings to capture with uncanny accuracy and good humour the mood of many of the incidents I have tried to describe.

M C

CHAPTER 1

Strictly a hobby

"Preserving worthy cars was always my prime motivation – bringing a neglected car back into use again."

My obsession with Jaguars began long before I bought my first one – a 1938 1½-litre saloon – but quite a long time after I had developed, at a very early age, a much less specific interest in cars in general and in their appearance. I was probably all of five years old when, in my juvenile way, I became quite dismayed by the way in which so many people seemed to travel around in neglected cars. It goes without saying that, like most youngsters, cars were already an abiding interest for me, and I already knew that when the time came for me to have one, it would be as smart as I could make it. There would be no bent wings and bumpers, tatty and scarred bodywork or smoke pouring out of the exhaust. 'My' car – or rather cars, because I already knew that I would want more than one – would become the object of my devotion and undivided attention! And that is more or less the way things have turned out.

I recall that one of my earliest ambitions was to own, not a Jaguar, but a Lagonda, preferably one with big headlights. In fact my parents became tired of me going on about it. Then one day another car appeared, and it was to change my destiny.

On my walk to school I had to pass a large detached house set in grounds of about half an acre and with a lawn that would have done credit to a golf course greenkeeper. The magnificent frontage was in full view of the road, but at the back and along both sides of the garden was a high chain-link fence, within which roamed about half a dozen savage-looking white beasts. We thought they were wolves, but in fact they were huskies, which probably made them an even greater danger to intruders.

The occupants of this elegant residence were a middle-aged couple, who were rumoured to be Russian aristocrats – they were certainly very wealthy. 'He' was often to be seen in the local shops, always dressed immaculately in suit and tie, regardless of the weather. He spoke with just a trace of an accent, was very pleasant to everyone he met, and he drove a Bugatti. 'She' was rarely seen at all, but she went everywhere in a very American-looking and chauffeur-driven car which I later discovered was an Invicta Black Prince – a rather ugly thing. Apart from this, very occasionally she could be seen parading in the garden, looking every bit the Hollywood film star. Everyone used to refer to her as the princess.

From time to time the most wonderful cars were to be seen at the house, a large green and cream Daimler being amongst the most regular callers. Then one day, parked outside, was the most beautiful car I had ever seen, an SS Jaguar 2½-litre drophead coupe, finished in gleaming blood red; the hood was folded back and it looked wonderful. That was the day I changed my loyalties and decided that I didn't want a Lagonda after all, I wanted an SS Jaguar. This was at about the time of the introduction of the Mk V and the XK120, so the red drophead was still effectively just about a current model.

From that day on I became a fervent Jaguar-spotter. A lot of them, of course, were newish cars in regular use, but increasingly as time went on I would discover them at the back of open-air used car lots, often with flat tyres and covered with grime. I desperately hoped that by the time I was old enough to drive there would still be some older Jaguars left to buy, so rapidly did they seem to be coming off the road.

I began what I called my Jaguar fund, putting aside some of my pocket money to save for the great day when it would buy me my first Jaguar. But that day was still a long way off, and other cars would have to come first – not because I preferred them, but because they were a means to an end.

The first car I bought, whilst still at school, was a Railton, and it cost me all of £5. It was parked in the driveway of a house close to home and it looked very sad. The owner told me that it would not pass the newly introduced MoT test due to a steering fault and that he had been offered a fiver for it from a scrap merchant, so if I was prepared to pay the same I could have the car. He gave me a week to remove it from his drive.

The next day a friend's father got me out of my predicament by offering to buy the Railton for £10, an offer I gladly accepted because by then it had dawned on me that otherwise I really didn't know what I could do with the car. So here was another £5 towards my Jaguar fund and, as it turned out, I had saved the Railton from the crusher, because after a long search for replacement steering parts the car eventually went back on the road.

Next came a Morris Eight of about 1935 vintage, which I bought from a porter at our local railway station for just 30 shillings (£1.50), which will give you some idea of the sort of state it was in. Nevertheless, I taught myself to drive in this contraption along a lane near home until its sagging chassis finally gave up the ghost and broke in two.

A few months before I was old enough to apply for my first driving licence I was broken-hearted at having to refuse the offer of a big SS saloon free of charge, simply because I had nowhere to keep it. It was either a 2½ or a 3½-litre from around 1938 and had been in recent use but, like a lot of cars at the time, it was being taken off the road because of the MoT test; many owners just didn't want to be bothered with it.

The big SS Jaguar made the journey to the breakers under its own power – one more example of why this was a bonanza time for the scrap men. Early Jaguars by now were commonplace in most yards, yet many of them, like this black SS, would have needed very little work to keep them on the road.

Determined that never again would I have to turn a car away for lack of space, I was able to rent a large lock-up garage in a secure place, hoping, of course, that another SS would soon show up. But instead, along came a 1929 Riley 9hp tourer with a fabric body. It was my first vintage car. The seller needed more space, as well as some cash, and gave me the choice of the 9hp or an earlier 11hp, both cars being in a similar, fairly rough condition and on offer at the same price. Even though it was a non-runner I chose the 9hp, and within a few days I had it running again, having confirmed that its engine, as had been promised, was indeed in sound condition.

But the car still needed a lot of work, including a new hood, a rewire, wheels repaired and various others jobs, all of which were beyond my capabilities and finances, and so a good home was found for the Riley. As part of the deal came a 1934 Austin Ten coupe, taxed and tested, which I thought would be an ideal car in which to learn to drive and take my test.

My father, however, decided on a more practical approach and arranged to instruct me in a Morris Minor 1000 convertible, in which I duly passed the test at the second attempt. He was also right about the Austin being a potential traffic hazard, for whilst driving it around the yard near my lock-up the clutch exploded into about a million pieces!

My very first car I was able to take on the road was a Standard Ten of about 1934 vintage, which ran very well until one of the rear wheels collapsed one evening, breaking a spring in the process. After this came a 1951 side-valve Humber Hawk, which I found was a lovely car to drive, only being spoilt by its rather tinny interior. I went all over the country in the Hawk and it never let me down.

But then, finally, came the big day when I became the proud owner of an attractive mid-green 1938 1½-litre SS Jaguar. I bought it off a garage forecourt for around £25 and it came

My road to Jaguar ownership was littered with the remains of bargain-priced lesser cars . . .

Throwing away those 'L' plates was a thrill, but then came the bombshell: in the world of insurance, youth and Jaguars just didn't mix.

with a rebuilt engine, a working radio and a long MoT certificate. How I looked forward to enjoying that car! Its cosy driving position, the big four-spoke steering wheel, the chubby gearlever in just the right place, and that wonderful, comprehensive dashboard. These were just some of the things which would bring me back time and time again to ownership of a Jaguar designed in the SS days.

But my delight in owning my first Jaguar was to be all too brief. Within a couple of days of taking over the car an envelope arrived by recorded delivery. I was to discover that insurance companies disliked young drivers in Jaguars. My insurance cover had been cancelled – and it would not be for the last time. But at least I could still work on them – the driving could come later.

What I needed now was a decent-sized and secure garage big enough for me to be able to work in comfort on at least two cars. The trouble was that premises of this sort were not only hard to come by, but also expensive. Imagine my delight, therefore, at being offered a workshop better than I could ever have dreamed of, on terms I could easily afford. A local company owned a purpose-built garage, but having disposed of all their lorries they no longer needed the place; long-term they planned to sell the site for development.

The workshop had offices above, and at the back was a concrete platform for loading vehicles, the underside of this platform forming a giant, if rather dark, storage area inside the garage. This space ran the full width of the building and was about 15 feet deep and 6 feet high, which meant that several cars could be stored there.

The workshop had sliding doors the full length of the front and could hold six very large cars with space to work around them, there was a concrete floor with a dry pit, overhead lifting gear and plenty of natural light, and the building stood in a spacious yard behind a strong fence. Normally, any garage business would have paid a fortune to rent or buy a place like this, especially as it was conveniently close to the railway station, but there was a problem to do with planning consent.

As it had been built as a private garage, the council would not allow any commercial enterprise to be carried on there. So the owners kept the offices above and rented me the garage underneath them for five years at a very low rental; they were to pay the rates and I would be responsible for the electricity bill and the water rate and would insure the place. To compensate for the low rental, I was either to pay for the servicing of their two company cars, or do this work myself. Both were Zephyr Mk IIIs and were only used locally, so as the cars were easy to work on, and I got on well with both users, this was no hardship.

One of the first things I did was to put in a slot meter for the electricity; it seemed to eat money, but when the bill came in I could empty the meter, pay the bill and pocket the change. The council were a bit awkward at first, not believing that I was just an enthusiast, but when they were sure I wasn't taking in paying jobs they were quite happy. After all, they were being paid rates!

My intention was to restore a 3½-litre Jaguar for my own eventual use and perhaps work on an XK over a longer period and, to help offset my overheads, possibly do up a vintage car or an older sportscar before reselling it. One problem I hadn't foreseen was that people using the station assumed I had opened a garage business; there were notes pushed under the door, visitors arrived most evenings and some even left cars outside the gates. I could have made a fortune, but I dared not risk antagonizing the local council, nor was I prepared to break the agreement with my landlord.

What did happen was that my green SS Jaguar was the first car to take up storage space when I discovered that it would not pass another MoT test because of a bodged chassis repair. After that, every unwanted Jaguar in the district seemed to turn up. Local scrap men, knowing of my interest, would often leave cars outside the gate. Usually they were SS types or perhaps Mk Vs, but occasionally it would be a Mk VII.

It seemed to me that Jaguars at that time were the most neglected cars in existence. Any model over about five years of age was valued at a fraction of its cost new and even then it

Welding a wing ~

WORKSHOP:
under the
loading-platform!

3½" Brake adjustment

Soon, my spacious garage was filled to overflowing, and every unwanted Jaguar in the district seemed to turn up.

had to be in excellent order if it was to find a buyer. The older cars, in particular those that looked dated, like the Mk Vs and the early postwar saloons, were virtually unsaleable, and the same applied to the prewar SS saloons.

It was always sad having to turn some of them away or to dispose of them. I did what I could to quite a lot of them, and in some cases passed them on to a fellow enthusiast, but some just had to go for scrap. Most of these cars would have been removed from their previous owners without any payment for them, and in some cases the owners would actually be charged for disposal, which was a common enough state of affairs at the time. In the main the cars which were brought to me commanded one of two prices: a fiver for a non-runner and a tenner for a runner. For the occasional really clean car, one that had recently been on the road, I would have been asked for perhaps £15. Motoring could be very cheap indeed in those days!

I was to spend just about every hour of my free time in that workshop over the next five years, and although it would be an exaggeration to say that it was a period of uninterrupted bliss, I thoroughly enjoyed working there, especially when at the end of a day's toil I had been able to give another previously unwanted Jaguar a new lease of life.

Preserving worthy cars was always my prime motivation – bringing a neglected car back into use again. It was never my intention to buy and sell cars for a profit, although if any of mine attracted the interest of a fellow enthusiast I would agree to sell it in order to finance the running of my premises and to help pay for the work I was undertaking on other cars. But every car I sold I made sure went to a caring owner, someone who would appreciate the car for its own qualities rather than for its bargain price, and on many occasions I have refused to sell Jaguars to someone I considered to be unsuitable, even if the price offered might have been attractive, and I wouldn't hesitate to do the same thing again.

The love of cars has always come first, and I do not regard interesting cars as a form of investment. In fact, in the past I have lost money in order to save cars that otherwise would have gone for scrap. Restoration has always been for me the most pleasurable part of old car ownership, and it may be an encouragement to others to know that I had no mechanical training for the jobs I have undertaken. It really isn't as difficult as it might seem, always provided, of course, that you are competent in a practical sense, and have a decent toolkit, the appropriate workshop manual if there is one, and a reasonable amount of suitable space in which to work.

Furthermore, I have never been constrained when carrying out restoration work by the idea that everything has to be returned to original specification. As I am not a *concours* fanatic, I am not obsessed by the concept of originality when, by departing from it, I can make the car more efficient, comfortable and safe. Why shouldn't an earlier model be given the benefit of improvements which only came along later? For example, I have put electric screen washers on 3½-litre saloons as well as applying flashing indicators to them very discreetly. I have installed all-synchro gearboxes in Mk IIs and XKs, converted an early Mk I from drum brakes to discs and carried out several conversions from automatic to manual transmission.

Obviously, the more work you undertake, the more skilled you should become in handling it, and it was not so very long before I found that overhaul of even the most complex engines was within my ability and there came a time when I could rebuild an XK engine without needing to look at the manual, then get it to start on the first or second turn and have it ticking over with not a trace of an oil leak. But gearboxes were another matter; these have always been things that I let other people put right for me, often at a very reasonable cost. Otherwise, there are few repairs, mechanical or structural, that I have not undertaken on the Jaguars I have owned, and I would urge anyone with a similar love of them not to be daunted by the prospect of undertaking quite major remedial work on their car. Not only will it be a lot cheaper than the alternatives, it can also be a lot of fun!

1934 *Airline*

SS·1 COUPE

CHAPTER 2

SS Jaguars

"Anyone considering restoration of one of these cars should bear in mind that the body is removable . . ."

Of all the Jaguars that have passed through my hands, the cars that carried the name of the 'Cat' as an appendage to their earlier SS identity have always had a particular appeal for me. It is not just that the first Jaguar I owned was one of these cars – though the first car often exerts a strong pull in an enthusiast's affection – but that they set out the ground rules for all the good things which subsequent Jaguars have represented. They were also, as I discovered, surprisingly nice cars to work on.

These were the cars, of course, with which Jaguar returned to car manufacture in 1945 and were in effect part of the 1940 range which had been prepared prior to the outbreak of World War Two. The only differences were a few minor updates and a subtle change of name, the 'SS' prefix having been dropped because of its unfortunate association with Nazi Germany.

There was to be a choice of three four-door saloons, two outwardly similar models with a six-cylinder engine of either 2,663cc (offering 102bhp) or 3,485cc (125bhp) for the 2½-litre and 3½-litre models, respectively, and a slightly shorter-wheelbase 1½-litre version housing a 1,775cc (65bhp) four-cylinder engine. Most of approximately 12,000 cars produced up to 1949 were saloons, about 7,000 of them remaining on the home market, but about 500 3½-litre and 100 2½-litre drophead coupes were made during the range's last two years of production.

Although of course the 1½-litre was no match for the six-cylinder models in performance terms, it was more than capable of holding its own against most 2-litre cars of the time, and even though a basic model was offered, most cars were turned out in SE trim, which meant that their standard fittings broadly mirrored those of the larger cars.

Despite being a prewar design, with such outdated features as a beam-type front axle and rod-operated brakes, buyers loved them, and for good reason, for they had a lot going for them. Somehow, Jaguar had performed something of a minor miracle in making them of quite heavy-gauge steel, so corrosion was not a problem for quite some time. The body structure formed from steel pressings welded together provided a shell of immense strength, which was mounted on the sturdy chassis by means of eight bolts on each side, while the massive front wings, running-boards and rear wings were also bolted to the main body.

The interiors were sumptuous, in the best traditions of leather and wood with a wool headlining and thick carpets. Most models had an advanced heating system, which was somewhat ambitiously called air conditioning, and a comprehensive set of instruments was set into the well-designed, polished wood dashboard. Such niceties as height adjusters for the front seats and quarter-lights operated by little handles offered standards of luxury that left other manufacturers in the cold.

The mechanics were simple and utterly reliable, and properly maintained these engines would last for many thousands of miles. But sadly, like so many subsequent Jaguars, all too often they were neglected, often because of the considerable cost of an oil change. Many of the cars also suffered from lack of lubrication of their steering joints and suspension, resulting in imprecise steering and a rather rough ride. Brakes were another neglected item, and although they were quite effective when properly set up, they could be quite dangerous when not maintained.

Over the years I have owned saloons of all three model sizes as well as a drophead and even an estate car conversion, and I must have carried out just about every job imaginable on them. Those cars were built like a giant construction kit, which meant that it was obvious where everything was meant to fit; it became a joy to work on them.

At the peak of my interest in them, in the early Sixties, rust was still not a serious concern, and such corrosion as I encountered was mainly confined to the door bottoms, under the rear wings, around the sides of the spare wheel cover and in the step panels below the doors, otherwise known as the front and rear body rockers.

But then I discovered a much more serious chassis rot problem with my 1938 1½-litre, which by then was 25 years old, and as I had no welding equipment at the time, the repair was beyond me. The problem was revealed when I took the car for its MoT test and a crude repair became visible when it was hoisted on a ramp. Rust had taken a hold on the rear chassis members, between the two spring hangers, pieces of angle iron of the type used for shelving having been bolted over the holes and the surrounding area liberally coated with gas tar. But although large pieces were missing, the sturdy chassis showed no danger of collapsing, and just as I was thinking that this would be the end of the little car, another enthusiast said he was keen to own it, and he duly completed the necessary repairs.

In exchange came an unfinished restoration project, a 3½-litre drophead coupe from about 1938. It had been stripped to the bare metal and the rust-free body coated with a grey primer. But at that point someone had lost interest and the masking tape had been on so long that it had almost become baked onto the chrome parts. The major problem was that the hood and its frame had been misplaced; the big chrome 'pram irons' were still there, but everything else was missing.

Despite being laid up for a considerable length of time, the big SS was soon coaxed back into life and proved to be in first-class mechanical order. An advertisement in *Exchange & Mart* led me to a similar car, which was being broken, but the greedy owner wanted about £25 just for a very tatty hood and frame, and as that was about the price I valued the entire car, the hood remained where it was. In the end, I just cleaned the SS, sheeted it up and stored it out of the way. A couple of years later it was sold to a garage owner from the Midlands, who took about five minutes to appraise the car. The following day he returned with drums of petrol and a set of trade plates and drove the car home.

The first time I tackled the removal of an overhead-valve cylinder head I chose to be really ambitious and got to work on a 2½-litre Jaguar, and the task proved to be so straightforward that it instantly removed any fears I might have had of 'complicated' Jaguar mechanicals. A local garage man had just told me that the owner of a postwar 2½-litre saloon wanted to get rid of the car quickly. He had been driving it along the busy A6 morning and night for years, but that day it had broken down – not for the first time – and that was it. I gave him £5 in exchange for the black 2½-litre with its grubby red interior, and as the seller handed over the logbook he said the £5 had been a bonus – he would have gladly given me the car!

Basically it was sound, the engine had good oil pressure, and even though it had a bad misfire, it didn't knock or rattle. But how that car even started, let alone ran, will always be a mystery to me. The points had burnt away completely, as had the plugs, the pistons in both carburettors were sticking, and the tappets were so far out of adjustment that the car had been running on about four-and-a-half cylinders.

After a proper service, and the first oil and filter change for many years, the car was much better, but there was still a misfire on one cylinder, which I put down to a burnt or sticking

A hole in the centre of one of the pistons proved to be the root cause of the problem.

valve. So I ordered a gasket set and went to work. It probably took about half a day to remove the head – it was my first one, remember, and I was in no hurry – but it didn't prove difficult at all, the main problem being the weight of the head itself.

To my surprise, the valves were alright, they just needed the carbon chipping off. It was caked on everywhere – valve stems, ports, pistons – and it took ages to clean the entire head and grind in the valves. I don't think I have ever seen such a build-up of 'coke' on a petrol engine. A hole in the centre of one of the pistons proved to be the root cause of the problem.

On both the 1½-litre and 2½-litre models, which share many engine components, the piston and conrod must be removed by squeezing them past the crankshaft and extracting them from the bottom as the conrod will not pass up through the bore.

Sumps are removable without disturbing the engine mounts or axle, but it proved to be a fiddly and very dirty job. But after this effort, the 2½-litre ran like a dream and I used it myself for a while, then the next owner kept it for many years; it had been his dream to own one for the pleasure he knew it would bring him.

That particular 2½-litre proved quite expensive to put right bearing in mind the minuscule prices at which old cars were changing hands at that time. The replacement piston, gaskets and other components would have cost around £20, then the plugs, points, filter, plus the 20 pints of oil necessary for a change would all have added considerably to the cost, without making any allowance for labour or overheads. The work I carried out certainly exceeded the value of the car in parts alone, which perhaps illustrates why these cars were so often quickly abandoned when something went wrong.

Engine removal on all these early-postwar Jaguars is very easy. It is a case of removing the bonnet and radiator, undoing all the bellhousing bolts from inside the car, then, after undoing the front mountings, lifting the engine and sliding it out at the front. It is just about the simplest of all Jaguar engine removals.

All the engines employ shell bearings, both the big-end and main bearing caps being held by nuts secured by split-pins. Although the manual may advise first of all removing the engine, I have removed sumps from both 1½-litre and 2½-litre cars with the engine *in situ*, and although I have not had cause to do so with a 3½-litre engine, I cannot imagine there would be any great problem. This means, of course, that the big-end shells can be examined with the engine in place.

Obviously, the engine must be removed prior to a stripdown, which is a very straight-forward procedure, no special tools being needed. Many engines will have been rebored in the past, and + .030in was the recommended rebore limit, after which liners and standard-size pistons were available from the factory. Grinding a crankshaft beyond .0040in was also not recommended, .0030in being considered the acceptable limit.

To the best of my knowledge, only standard pistons were fitted, giving a compression ratio of the order of 6.5:1. The six-cylinder engines used Duralumin conrods, which were not bushed, factory exchange rods being the only answer in the event of wear. For some reason, the 1½-litre used steel rods with bushed little-ends, and I have been told that the conrods from a 1½-litre can be used in the 2½-litre engine. I have never tried this, but the dimensions would appear to be the same.

The camshafts are very robust and are quite easily removed for examination or replacement after first removing the rocker gear. On the larger cars the rev-counter drive is taken from the camshaft. Timing chain replacement is another simple task; just be sure to mark both chain wheels before removing the camshaft chain wheel. The 1½-litre cars use a single chain and have a tensioner fixed to the inside of the timing cover. The larger cars have a duplex chain and have tensioners mounted on the engine block within the cover.

On all three engines it is possible to adjust the oil pressure by means of a screw concealed by a domed nut on the side of the oil filter assembly body; clockwise increases the pressure and anti-clockwise decreases it, and at normal operating temperature an acceptable reading would be about 50 to 60psi at around 2,500rpm. Reliable sources have told me that in the past, shady dealers became expert at obtaining good pressure readings from worn engines, and it is just possible that their expertise has been passed on!

To rebuild an engine completely should not take too many hours because there are no hidden complications, and even the valve and ignition timing can be done without special tools. As for all Jaguars, a good manual is a 'must', and although original ones for these late prewar and early postwar models may be few and far between, at least these are forgiving engines, and a small error might at worst mean a failure to start, whereas with the later overhead-camshaft engines the result could well be a set of bent valves.

With one exception, every early Jaguar I owned required attention of some sort, but this one car gave me an insight into what it must have been like to own one of these cars from new. At a time when I thought I had no space for another car, a local person whom I knew only as the owner of an Aston Martin DB4 called to ask me if I would care to have a look at a 1947 Jaguar he wished to dispose of. Although I had lived in the district for several years, I had never seen this car, so this came as a pleasant surprise.

It turned out to be a 3½-litre saloon finished in silver grey with a red leather interior, it stood in a heated garage that would have made a nice house, and I was talking to its original owner. He had bought his dream car two years after the war, had used it regularly for a few years, then had kept it as a pampered pet. Now he had decided to sell it, and he thought that I would be a fit person to own it.

It looked to be about two years old, there was not a scratch or mark anywhere, the chrome was sparkling and the interior unmarked, the back seats having never even been sat on. The only non-original things were the silver stove enamelling on the wheels, which were fitted with new tyres, the new battery, a new exhaust and the Trico electric screen washers. The car had always been taxed and in its semi-retirement it covered just a couple of hundred miles a year on the road. The car came with the original bill of sale and service history, confirming a genuine mileage of just over 20,000. The price was £65, which was not negotiable – it was a case of take it or leave it. When I collected the car the next day I noticed that it was still taxed for ages and the fuel tank was filled to the brim.

The next week I did a tour of Wales in my beautiful new Jaguar, which went like the wind, with power aplenty, not a squeak or rattle to be heard, and even the brakes worked properly. On those quiet roads I could have been back in the summer of 1948, and although I was only to use it for special occasions and no-one ever sat on that back seat while I had it, I have never enjoyed ownership of a car so much. That winter I had to make an unexpected cross-country dash in blizzard conditions and the big car performed magnificently.

The gearbox on these early cars was in my opinion one of the best fitted to any Jaguar, with a smooth and precise change and well thought out ratios. After a while, some of the early 'boxes developed bearing noise, in particular on the larger models, and the synchromesh on second and third also became a little noisy. But these things apart, the 'boxes were strong and long-lived, and the only one I came across with a serious fault was as a result of damage through abuse.

I have already indicated that gearbox internals are something I like to leave to the specialists, but I was interested to watch an expert rebuild one of these 'boxes and to hear him declare that it was one of the most straightforward 'boxes he had ever worked on.

During the period when I owned these cars, very few owners would have gone to the expense of replacing the clutch or gearbox on one of them, despite both operations being quite easy. However, I did the job on a 2½-litre which had been given to me after failing its MoT test but was otherwise generally in first-class condition.

It was an ivory-coloured saloon with a clean red interior and it had failed the test due to excessive wear in the kingpins. It was also suffering from clutch slip when the owner dumped it on me. When I jacked up the front I found it was possible to rattle the wheels about, all the symptoms certainly pointing to worn kingpins. But the trouble turned out to be play in the front hub bearings, for which the remedy seemed to be a simple adjustment, then packing the bearings with grease.

Simple the task might have been in theory, but in practice it meant hours of poking inside the splined hub to remove the split-pin securing the castellated nut, the job of lining everything up to fit a new pin being only slightly less difficult. But at least it was a far easier and simpler job than doing the kingpins and bushes.

The car now had a valid MoT certificate, so the next problem was the worn clutch as well as a very noisy reverse gear – driving the car backwards produced a noise rather like a steam hammer in operation!

The gearbox on these cars is extracted through the inside of the car after taking out the front seats, carpets and floorboards and removing the gearbox cowl. This exposes the bellhousing and the propshaft bolts are readily accessible. It is advisable to disconnect the exhaust downpipes as the engine must be supported under the sump before removal of the 'box; the rear of the engine will have to be raised slightly to enable the box to clear the chassis. Removing the 'box is supposed to be a one-man task, but the 'boxes are quite heavy, and in such a restricted space the job is much easier with some help.

On this particular 2½-litre I fitted a good used 'box, which cost just a few pounds, and I remember fitting new front and rear seals, which was a simple operation with the gearbox out on the floor. Removing the clutch assembly proved to be quite awkward because of the difficulty of having to crouch under the bulkhead to remove bolts which had been well tightened. The assembly is also rather heavy, and it may be difficult to remove it from the dowels whilst supporting the weight – there is no room for a helper in there – so I put down some cardboard and let the unit drop to the floor – better than crushed fingers!

It is important to properly line up the gearbox before final seembly, the best method being to operate the clutch pedal a dozen or so times with top gear selected, then tighten up the

Removing the gearbox is supposed to be a one-man task, but . . .

bellhousing bolts. Clutch adjustment is by means of a screw and locknut on the side of the gearbox casing, and free play should be about ¾ to 1in. The clutch pedal is mounted on the gearbox bellhousing, and adjustment is also provided for the angle of the pedal. The propshaft should have grease nipples for both the front universal joint and the splined joint, so this is an excellent chance to lubricate both of them before the floorboards and trim are refitted.

The rod-operated brakes fitted to early Jaguars were about the most effective mechanical braking systems available at the time. The linkage was designed to be fully compensating, the idea being that any adjustment of the operating rods would only be necessary after a high mileage. Each of the large drums has an adjuster screw at the back, and the handbrake may be adjusted by means of a rod accessible from under the car.

Overhaul of the system should include renewing worn clevis pins and yokes on the linkage and adjusting the rods to the correct lengths. The manual will show a proper procedure for this operation, but it is most important to set the system up properly; remember that all the rods are designed to pull, not push. I had a most unpleasant experience with a 1½-litre saloon when the need to brake hard resulted in the rear wheels locking up. I was able to get the car mobile again only after using the wheel hammer to free off the linkage. This is how I came to know about brake rods which were fitted wrongly! This is quite a common mistake, I gather, because it is one which is not always apparent during normal use. Indeed, the brakes on my 1½-litre had worked quite well until I had to pull up in a hurry. When they are properly set up, these brakes are capable of stopping these heavy cars within a reasonable distance, but at speed it is a little different, and anyone who has had to brake in a hurry will probably confirm my claim that quite often this means standing up in the seat!

As I have owned several of these cars which had been properly maintained, including that one with the incredibly low mileage, I am able to say that the suspension system is capable of providing an excellent ride, along with good roadholding. The low-mileage 3½-litre I owned gave me a ride free of any vibration or road shock, the only fault I ever found being slight axle tramp on very bumpy roads, which was only to be expected from any car with a beam front axle.

This same car, when driven hard, was an absolute pleasure, the back end always feeling 'alive', yet under control and the suspension well able to cope with road conditions in all weathers. I felt very confident in this car, whereas in models which had suffered the usual wear in the suspension and steering, taking a bend at anything over about 50mph could shake my confidence. Many former owners have criticized the cars for poor roadholding and atrocious brakes, but these faults were not inherent in the cars' design, they were the result of the usual old Jaguar problems, abuse and neglect.

Though of fairly basic design, the suspension system is quite effective with its traditional solid axles front and rear, both mounted on leaf springs and damped by lever-type hydraulic shock absorbers. The units are fixed to the chassis-frame and then connected to the axle by short link rods fitted with rubber bushes. Removal is quite easy, access to the rear units being via the inspection panel which forms the boot floor. Provision is made for topping-up the shock absorbers, but not for their adjustment.

The front axle is easily removed for repairs, and on the only occasion on which I had to replace kingpins I found that taking the axle off made the job a lot easier. On that occasion I stripped the axle of back plates, hubs, etc and delivered it to a local firm that made and repaired springs. The next day I collected the axle with its new pins and I seem to remember

Anyone who has had to brake in a hurry will probably confirm that quite often this means standing up . . .

a charge of just £3 to fit my own parts. This company also reconditioned leaf springs and was able to retemper them, fit new leaves, bushes, etc, in fact make them as good as new, all at a very reasonable cost. I used their services on many occasions and I find it sad that today few if any firms of this sort still exist, which is a great loss to modern day enthusiasts.

According to the manuals, removing a rear axle is simple, just a case of drawing off the rear splined hubs, removing the backplate, then sliding the axle out under the wheelarch!. But anyone who has tried to draw off a hub fitted to a keyway and taper will know that it is not possible without a press. My local agent, with whom I was on good terms, told me that they had rarely been able to remove an axle in one piece; cutting the casing with a blow torch and fitting a new unit was the only way.

An otherwise sound 2½-litre saloon had backlash in the axle which was so bad that with the car jacked up and in gear it was possble to move the wheel about 6in before the play was taken up. I decided to change the axle. A good unit was found in a breaker's yard, the cost being about £4. The scrap man insisted that the only way to remove it was to cut both chassis and springs. How right he was.

But still thinking I knew better, I bought an expensive three-armed puller and attempted to draw the rear hubs off my 2½-litre, but with the puller almost at breaking point and the cherry red hub being tapped with a sledge hammer, the only thing to give was the puller. So I borrowed a cutting torch and removed the axle in several bits.

The replacement axle was taken to the local agents where they just about managed to get it on their press, and at a pressure of around 30 tons the first taper broke with a bang like a WW1 gun; the second one was not quite as stubborn. Having got the new axle under the car, it was a matter of minutes to refit those hubs, a sharp contrast to the trouble and expense of removing them. Replacing that axle was one of the dirtiest, heaviest and most unpleasant jobs I have done on any Jaguar, and it is not one I would wish to do again.

A Burman Douglas steering assembly is used on all three models, and the only adjustment possible is to reduce the end float of the inner column. After removal from the car, a lengthy operation which includes the partial removal of the dashboard, the steering assembly can be dismantled for examination and the renewal of worn parts.

The horn assembly combines the trafficator, dip and, in some cases, the advance/retard switches. This arrangement, often called a manette control, is fixed to a long tube containing the wires, the tube passing through the centre of the steering column. Quite often, this inner tube can be the cause of frayed wires and possibly minor short-circuits.

Returning to the subject of chassis corrosion, although on my only Jaguar with rust here it was confined to the narrow rear sections close to the spring mountings, subsequently I was able to examine other cars with more extensive corrosion at the rear of the chassis, an area which is always difficult to examine without the use of a ramp. Another rust point is in the centre, on the outer frame, where the body mounts are welded on. However, anyone considering restoration of one of these cars should bear in mind that the body is removable, and that the design of the frame allows for welded repairs without the need for complex sections of new metal.

The 1½-litre cars have a single-pipe exhaust system, mostly with just one silencer, whereas the two six-cylinder cars employ an identical twin-pipe system with four silencers. Apart from the downpipes, the layouts use quite simple bends, and I have fabricated almost complete systems for these cars using readily available pipes and boxes. They are, in fact, amongst the most straightforward of all Jaguar exhaust systems.

Bodywork, being of quite substantial thickness, resisted rust very well. The average age of the cars I owned was around 15 years, and even at such an age rust had not taken a serious hold. The area where I most frequently encountered problems was around the spare wheel cover, where mud and water had collected and attacked the hinge mounting points and the spare wheel tray. Rust also took hold under the rear wings, and for some reason holes would appear in the arch where the rear armrests bolt on. I have also encountered cars where the

wing has resisted rust, but the rear quarter panel on to which the wing bolts has corroded.

Door bottoms were another problem area, and rot was common in the little rocker panels that fit between the running-board and doorstep. The panel hidden by these rockers, on to which the running-boards are bolted, could also rot away unseen, and rot in the centre pillar developed from here, although not until some years later did I come across a car with serious centre pillar rust. These problems apart, about the only other rust areas were around the wire on the rolled wing edges and damage caused by a leaking sunroof or blocked drain tubes.

Not so long ago I had the opportunity to appraise a 3½-litre saloon dating from around 1947 which had just emerged from about 20 years of dry storage, and I was quite surprised to find how many parts had been affected by serious rust. Many of the rotted parts of this car were obviously areas that had been disguised with filler many years ago.

On both sides, the rear quarter panels, to which the wings bolt, had almost completely rusted away and most of the inner wings were in a similar condition. All the doors had serious rot and would have been beyond repair, both the centre pillars had broken away and about the bottom 6in had rusted to nothing. The screen pillars had also rusted away and only the windscreen itself had prevented the roof from collapsing at the front. The entire edge of both front wings had been eaten away, leaving a jagged edge between the wing and the beaded edge. Probably the only two panels on the car that were of any use were the bootlid and the bonnet. In other words, it was what I once heard a scrap man so accurately describe as a 'shovel job'.

If I were buying one of these early Jaguars today, unless I knew the history of the car being offered, I would much prefer to buy one in need of restoration so that I could see what it was really like before it had been 'rebuilt'. Like most other Jaguar models, these once unwanted cars have become quite saleable and in consequence have attracted the attention of the less scrupulous. In fact, an artful bodger will have little difficulty in making one look very presentable to the inexperienced.

The recent history of such a car I encountered is a good example of what can happen. A 3½-litre saloon which had been in store for years and was not a particularly good example suddenly acquired a coat of instant synthetic paint similar to its original silver grey and a new MoT certificate before appearing at a 'classic' auction. I viewed the car out of curiosity, and from a distance it looked nice, but the interior was shabby, the engine belched fumes, and something I noticed which presumably others had not was that the entire underside of the car was covered in a thick layer of red rust. Obviously, this car had stood on a damp floor for years, but even so it sold, only to appear again at the premises of a dealer in thoroughbred cars.

By now, steam-cleaning had removed the surface rust, the underside had been coated in black paint, as had the engine block, the interior had been treated with rejuvenator, the bodywork was now two-toned with black and the worn engine had been dosed with chemicals. It was for sale once more, stripped of its original registration number, and offered with a service history. The dealer relieved the car's new owner of quite a sum of money.

Non-existent brakes, due to the linkage being rusted solid, was the first problem, but other faults, all MoT failure points, soon appeared. The engine started to rumble, then the rust began to break through, but in the meantime our friendly 'enthusiast dealer' had gone out of business. In the end, the 3½-litre was sold at a tremendous loss as a restoration project. It was a very expensive lesson for a nice person who had been taken in by cosmetic appearances, and sadly there will be a lot of similar cars out there just looking for a new owner!

The lesson is an obvious one. If you're not familiar with a car, don't even think of appraising it alone. Take someone along who knows exactly what to look for. If you are not already a member of one of the excellent Jaguar car clubs, as a potential recruit don't be afraid to ask for advice, but perhaps better still, join one anyway and meet and discuss things with your fellow members.

But despite the horror story I have just related, ownership of an early Jaguar can be an enjoyable experience. Remember that apart from serious body rot, any person with enthusiasm and a reasonable amount of equipment can do most things on these models. Even the interior trim, which may look quite complex, is really of very basic construction, and it is only jobs like the recovering of upholstery which are likely to be beyond the capabilities of most of us, and I hope that the chapter on interior renovation towards the back of this book will help to guide you along the right lines.

In total I must have owned around 15 different SS and early Jaguar cars, and that does not include those I did not use on the road. Amongst them was an SS 3½-litre drophead coupe and there was the unusual estate car which I kept in storage for quite some time. I only regret that I failed to photograph most of these cars at the time because they were certainly amongst the most enjoyable that I have had through my hands, and from time to time even today I hanker after owning another one – perhaps a silver 3½-litre with gleaming red interior!

Two of my cars of the past deserve further mention, not just because they were unusual, but because sadly neither was worth the high cost of restoration. The first was a 1938 2½-litre SS Jaguar saloon, which had been rebadged as a Jaguar 3½-litre, possibly to make it seem 10 years younger. The bodywork had also been modified in a very professional way, both running-boards having been removed and the ends of the front wings rounded off, very much in the style of a Triumph roadster. In place of the running-boards, panels with neat louvres had been made which neatly blended the front wings to the rears, running parallel with the chassis and fitting up close to the bottom of the doors. With its good quality repaint in silver, the car looked quite distinctive and somewhat unusual. Apparently the previous owner had admitted having bought it as a 'cheap flash car', and had neglected it badly and

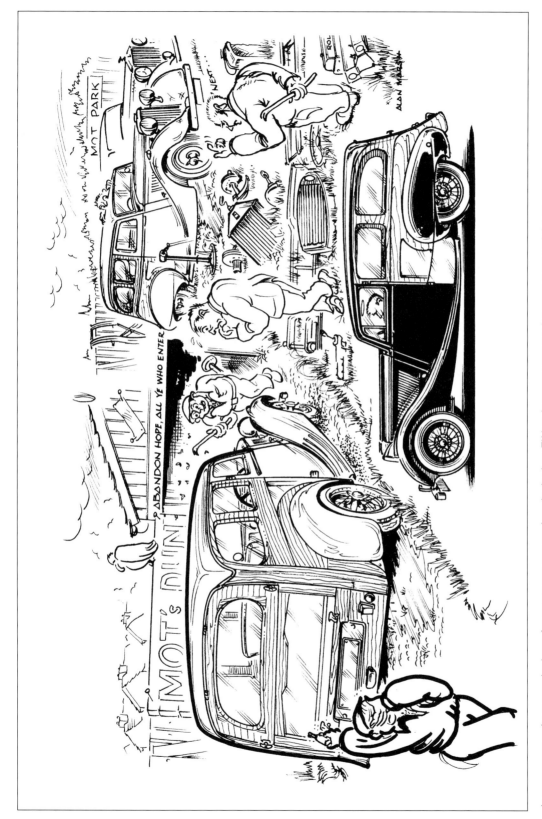

Jaguars were quite a popular base for estate car conversions in the late Fifties, but some were a lot more successful than others.

allowed it to run so low on oil that its engine had seized; I always imagined him to have been some sort of spiv character.

The car's conversion was not purely visual, though. It had obviously been done a long time earlier, and it included conversion to hydraulic brakes, the system using the original drums and backplates with hydraulic wheel cylinders, and the existing brake pedal had been adapted to operate the reservoir. Sadly, this unusual looking car ended up at the breaker's; it was simply not worth the bother or expense of replacing the engine.

Another unusual car, which was a regular sight in our neighbourhood in the late Fifties, was a Jaguar 1½-litre with an estate car body, an elegant conversion that had been carried out by Angel Motor Bodies, of Manchester. In my opinion, this firm's bodies, which were built from hardwood, were the only ones to blend with the lines of the car rather than appearing to have been tacked on as an afterthought. They had put bodies on a wide variety of vehicles, from everyday Fords and Austins to Rovers, Alvises, Armstrong Siddeleys and even a Bentley, and I knew that they had also produced other early Jaguars and later, I believe a Mk VII, although I never saw one.

Later, an Angel-bodied Jaguar came my way in unusual circumstances. Unexpectedly, a garage owner offered me, free of charge, a large quantity of early Jaguar parts, many of them brand new. The only conditions were that I would take them away quickly and that I would also remove from his premises another car which was described as being 'useful for bits'.

My benefactor had arranged for the spares to be loaded onto his large trailer, and a friend of mine drove the 1956 Humber Snipe I was running at that time, which happened to have towing gear, and I took along a Jaguar 3½-litre saloon with which to tow away the other Jaguar. Imagine my delight at finding this to be a 1947 2½-litre with an Angel estate body.

It looked a bit rough, but not until I got it over the pit later did I realize what a sorry state it was in. Both the rear doors had been removed, as had the wooden floor, the purpose having been to fit a small crane, which had been bolted through the chassis. During its hard life the bolt holes had stretched and stretched and such was the damage, further aggravated by years of rust, that the chassis was on the point of collapse. With the rear doors back in place and a good clean, the car looked quite presentable, and all of the steel bodywork was fairly sound, while the timbers, apart from slight cosmetic damage, were completely free of rot, as was the fabric roof.

But the only way to have saved the car would have been to fit another chassis because the damage was so bad that welding was out of the question. The estate car stood in the corner of the workshop for over a year and then, after much thought and a certain amount of heart-searching, it went for scrap. I was sad to see it towed away, because I always regretted having to give up on one of these fine cars, but my one consolation has always been that I was able to save many more from the cutting torch at a time when few people appreciated them.

3½ Litre Saloon

CHAPTER 3

Mk Vs, Mk VIIs and their successors

"Perhaps it was that they were using better-quality steel for the Mk VIIs than on the later Mk VIIIs and IXs."

During the early postwar years Jaguar formulated a lot of exciting plans for the future, but the problem was that it would take time to bring them to fruition, and in the meantime the existing cars, being essentially prewar models reincarnated, were becoming seriously out of date from a design standpoint. Clearly, something had to be done to plug the gap before the first truly new cars and engines were ready for production, and the answer, of course, came in the form of the Mk V, which was announced late in 1948.

At this time, car manufacturers were introducing some fairly unusual styles, far removed from anything they had offered previously, but you could tell instantly that the Mk V was a Jaguar. Most of the body panels looked remarkably similar to those of the previous models, and so they should because this was very much an interim model, combining the old 2½-litre and 3½-litre engines in a new chassis with independent front suspension and hydraulic brakes.

With its rather clumsy double bumpers, the Mk V had been given a distinctly transatlantic look and people tended to either love them or loathe them. Frankly, I hated them, and I declined several offers of nice examples. One of the most irritating features for me was the dashboard, with its stylized instruments, which I thought were so un-Jaguar and more suitable for an Austin Atlantic or perhaps a GM-inspired Vauxhall. In fact, to my mind, not until the first XJ-S appeared would Jaguar produce another such unpleasant set of instruments.

But appearance apart, these were nice cars to drive, and the torsion-bar independent suspension offered an excellent ride and good roadholding, with none of the axle tramp which had been a feature of the earlier cars. The brakes, too, were much better, and the interior, though not quite as cosy, was much lighter and seemed more spacious.

This was also the first Jaguar to be offered without wire wheels; the 670 x 16in tyres of the Mk V were mounted on a set of pressed-steel wheels. As previously, Jaguar offered both a four-door saloon and a drophead coupe, and during their three years in production more than 9,000 saloons and getting on for 1,000 coupes were sold, nearly 8,000 of the cars in total being badged as 3½-litre models. Of the coupes, only about 25 of them came out with the 2½-litre engine. Experience with the previous models had confirmed to Jaguar that their customers preferred bigger engines, and any thoughts of offering for sale a four-cylinder version of the forthcoming twin-overhead-camshaft engine were quickly and wisely abandoned.

My prejudice against the Mk V meant that my experience of this model would be quite limited, but although I cannot claim to have actually owned one in the conventional owner-driver sense, I did drive one of them quite regularly and I have to admit that I quite enjoyed using the car. Of course, because the model was relatively shortlived, it quickly became unwanted on the used car market, and from the mid-Fifties you could pick one up for a very

The Mk V was a Jaguar I decided I could do without, a feeling that was considerably reinforced when the elegant Mk VII came along.

reasonable cost. In fact, during that period yesterday's Jaguar became about as saleable as yesterday's newspaper.

My first encounter with a Mk V was when I was offered one as 'an old car to play around with' at about the time I was learning to drive. It belonged to a company, but had sat neglected in a garage alongside bits of broken and abandoned machinery and old oil drums. The tyres were flat, the windows and sunroof had been left open, pigeons had soiled the white paint and red seats and altogether this 2½-litre looked very sad indeed. It was less than 10 years old and had had only one owner, but even as a gift it was of no interest to me.

Then, during the early Sixties I had custody of a 3½-litre saloon, which originally had also been a company car, but was now being disposed of by its second owner, who had been unable to part-exchange it for the nearly new Jaguar 2.4 he was buying. So he loaned it to me in the hope that I would either buy it or find a new owner for it. The car was black with a brown interior – just about the most dreary colour combination available – but it was immaculate, having covered a very low mileage. It also drove like a dream and possessed that remarkable top gear tractability that I had enjoyed so much in the earlier cars.

Another Mk V was given to me because the owner was moving and wanted to get rid of it quickly; it had stood for a couple of years because of a broken halfshaft. This car will always remain a mystery to me because when I lifted the bonnet, there sat an OHC engine, looking very much as if it had always been there. The last owner could not offer any clue because he had bought the car in about 1958 with the same engine and had thought that all Jaguars had engines like that!

This 3½-litre litre was another black car, this time with a scruffy red interior, and as it showed no signs of a quick engine transplant I can only assume that the engine had either been fitted at the factory or it had been the work of an official Jaguar agent early in the car's life. Although I had the engine running, the clutch plate had rusted to the flywheel and the car generally had deteriorated to such a state through standing idle that in the end it went for scrap. Fairly recently I had the considerable pleasure of driving a newly restored example, which was smooth, relatively silent and with ample power, and it quite renewed my interest in Mk Vs. Maybe they weren't such bad cars after all!

But the Mk VII was on a different plane altogether. I loved that car from the moment I set eyes on it and it is easy to see why the model made such an impact when it was launched – superbly elegant, offering sportscar performance and, once again, wonderful value.

My first Mk VII came direct from a main agent's compound. It was normally their policy to dispose of all trade-ins via an auction, but on this occasion I was given the chance to buy a car for my own use. Most of the cars for disposal were Jaguars, the majority of them being Mk VIIs, VIIIs or IXs, although there were also a couple of XKs, the odd Mk I and a few older and obsolete models that were clearly destined for a 'banger' auction, whereas the newer cars would be sent to one of the more reputable sales.

At that time, most Jaguars seemed to leave their first owner after about two years, and I recall a salesman telling me that later XKs and early E-types were just 'unwanted lumps'! The Mk VII I chose was a 1952 model in ivory with a sumptuous red interior. The body was grimy and somewhat neglected, but it was free of corrosion, and mechanically the car was good. In fact the only fault I could find was a rattling timing chain. I think it was the red interior, which I think always looks good in a Jaguar, which proved the deciding factor, plus the fact that the car still had a current MoT certificate, not having been standing around for as long as the majority of the cars in the compound. So I drove my new Mk VII home, having paid about £35 for it.

Perhaps my prejudice against the Mk V was misplaced because later, after working on other people's cars, I decided that they were not so bad after all.

After a couple of days' hard work the car had been transformed, in fact it would have looked quite at home parked outside some top flight hotel in the South of France. The cleaned and polished bodywork had revealed no serious dents, the chromework was perfect, while the interior needed nothing more than vacuuming out and a light clean.

A service, with an oil change and new filter and adjustment of the top chain, had revealed only one slight fault – a cracked servo pipe, the replacement of which had done wonders for the car's braking efficiency. The 11-year-old Mk VII was a delight to drive, and as the Mk IX derivative had only recently gone out of production, my car looked far from dated. Even today I rate the Mk VII high up amongst my favourite Jaguars.

On the first occasion I drove it to the local garage to fill the twin fuel tanks a passer-by stopped to admire the car. It turned out that he had owned a similar model, and in return for a lift home he offered me a continental touring kit and an official workshop manual. Refusing all payment for these generous gifts, he also offered a piece of sound advice about Mk VIIs. They could prove to be very light at the back end, he told me, and he said that he had always carried a bag of sand at either side of the boot, which had helped to keep the tail end on the road when cornering fast.

Only a few days later, I was coming out of a bend quite quickly when, despite the dry road and the Mk VII's good tyres, the back end let go, and as I fought to regain control I remember thinking I wonder if this would have happened if I had heeded the good advice and slipped a bag of sand into each side of the boot? From that day on, the Mk VII never went anywhere without a pair of sandbags in the back, and I never lost the tail end again.

I hope no-one would accuse me of being a reckless driver, but I have always enjoyed driving hard under the right conditions, and the Mk VII was a car I learned to respect.

Despite the Mk VII's good tyres, suddenly the back end let go and I thought maybe I should have put that bag of sand in the boot after all.

Maybe they leaned somewhat on corners, and yes, perhaps they were a little light at the back, but properly handled they could be driven and cornered swiftly and safely. After all, the car had been designed as a fast and luxurious long-range tourer, and this was a job it performed very well indeed.

A few weeks after I had bought it, my car's clutch started to slip, and this was when I got to know Mk VIIs very well indeed. Despite their bulk, I found them quite easy and a pleasure to work on. If it becomes necessary, the engine and gearbox should be removed as a unit, and with the bonnet, radiator and grille removed there is ample room for manoeuvre. Ignore tips about lifting the engine forward, undoing the bellhousing bolts and leaving the gearbox dangling from the bulkhead. Also, don't be tempted to cut the floor in an attempt to split the unit and remove the 'box from underneath. Oh yes, it has been tried, so when examining a car, look for past attempts at similar butchery.

Of course, engine removal is only necessary for a major overhaul, or to gain access to the clutch, most other jobs being possible with the engine still in place. The sump will come off quite easily if big-end shells have to be replaced, and things like timing chains and pistons can be removed once the head is off.

The twin SU type H6 carburettors have an automatic choke which, like many Jaguar auto chokes, likes to stay on longer than necessary, so on my Mk VIIs (and some other models) I fitted a manual switch with a warning light to control the operation of the choke. In order to draw fuel from the twin tanks a pair of electric pumps are mounted under the rear of the car, and although there is a changeover switch enabling either tank and its pump to be brought into use, many cars have been run on just one tank for years, for a variety of reasons.

The Mk VIIs were equipped with the standard Moss gearbox, which with its slow, laborious change and long movement seemed more suited to an agricultural vehicle than a high-speed luxury car. Many would agree that these 'boxes, which lasted until well into the Sixties, were sufficiently disappointing to have put off quite a lot of potential owners. But this criticism apart, they proved to be long-lived, even when neglected. Also, most Mk VIIs were equipped with overdrive, and an automatic gearbox became available later in production.

The clutch is hydraulic, easily adjusted and for most owners long-lasting, but those who got into the habit of starting off in third or even, would you believe, top gear, soon discovered that this lazy technique did nothing to improve clutch life. Incidentally, the Mk VII's split propshaft is easily removed for repairs, etc.

The rear axle is mounted above the road springs, with the chassis passing over the top. The suggested way of removal is to draw off the hubs, remove the backplates, then slide the axle out from one side. However, I found this to be a tiresome operation involving shims and

Whenever you are checking one over, take a good look under the rear wheelarches – recognized as a weak point on the Mk VII.

oil seals, as well as having to dismantle the brakes, and I discovered that it was easier to undo the rear spring shackles, lower the complete assembly, then remove the axle under the back of the car. This also makes replacement far easier – securing the axle to the springs, jacking it into place, refitting the spring shackles and then tightening the U-bolts, etc. The only occasion on which I had to replace a Mk VII axle was because of a noisy crownwheel, and I found it to be quite an easy operation from a technique point of view, although I have to admit that it did involve some heavy work and it was certainly a dirty job.

The Mk VII's front suspension is an improved version of the system first used on the Mk V, an efficient layout which involves the use of torsion bars, wishbones, telescopic shock absorbers and an anti-roll bar. The torsion bars run along the inner face of the chassis and are mounted so as to allow adjustment of the ride height, and the suspension system makes liberal use of rubber bushes. The parts most prone to wear are the upper and lower balljoints, because although grease nipples are fitted, they are not easy to reach and therefore this particular service operation is so often neglected. But with its suspension properly maintained, the Mk VII was able to provide standards of ride and roadholding that other manufacturers were unable to achieve until years later.

During my involvement with Mk VIIs, I never encountered any serious rust problems on the substantial chassis. However, if I were looking at one now, I would examine very carefully the rear end where it sweeps up over the axle, as well as the narrow sections that continue to the rear of the car. As with earlier Jaguar chassis, the use of box sections allows for easy welding repairs, always assuming that you can actually reach the part that needs to be welded!

Some years ago, a friend bought from a private seller what appeared to be a very nice Mk VII in red with off-white upholstery – I thought the colour combination suited the car very well. But it was not long before he realized he had a problem. Every time he made a sharp left turn the nearside front tyre screeched horribly and tyre wear became dreadful; fortunately, he had been able to discover a seemingly endless supply of 670x16in tyres and wheels from local scrapyards!

When I took a close look at the car, the first thing I noticed was that another front wing had been fitted. Although it was clearly a secondhand one, it looked to be sound, and there was a good colour match. Then I peered underneath the car and discovered that there was a slight vertical crease just behind the front suspension mounting posts. With the whole vehicle out of alignment it would have been impossible to line up the steering properly, so in an attempt to make the car driveable someone had packed the top wishbone shims with washers and taken the nearside track rod to the limit of its adjustment. Strangely, in the circumstances, the car steered well, and it was just the left-hand turns which posed the problem.

When confronted with it, the person who had sold the car to my friend expressed ignorance and innocence, but the truth of the matter was that the car had been written-off following a collision with a concrete bollard. So after being paid out for the car, the owner had bought it back cheaply as salvage and had then had a dangerous bodge job done by a dodgy repairer. Then, not satisfied with having gained another couple of extra months' use out of the car, and becoming tired at having to buy so many secondhand tyres, he had decided to extract a final few pounds out of the Jaguar by selling it on. I seem to recall that the car had cost my friend about £65, which was a fair price for a usable Mk VII at the time, but he decided to cut his losses and sold the car for scrap, insisting that it was cut up. This time it was!

Over the years I have seen quite a few Jaguars with hidden faults and in a dangerous condition being offered for sale by private individuals who had gone to great trouble to hide the truth. I often wonder how such people, who in the past were quite willing to unload a potential deathtrap for perhaps £30 to £40, would behave today with values up in the hundreds and thousands of pounds! At least these days everyone is supposed to be more safety-conscious, but it always pays to be vigilant.

Back to the Mk VII, the steering is through a recirculating ball-type unit mounted on one side of the chassis, with an idler box on the other side, a drop arm being connected to the underside of each of the units. The two drop arms are connected by a track rod, the outer ends of which being attached to the steering arms by means of short tie-rods. The steering box can be removed for repair or adjustment without having to disturb the column, but the idler unit has no facility for overhaul, so a replacement unit must be fitted when wear occurs. Most of the steering parts are easily accessible on this well-designed and efficient system.

The Mk VII uses a fully hydraulic Girling braking system with a servo unit and 12in diameter drums all round, the front brake shoes being self-adjusting, while the rears have an adjuster nut. Both the master-cylinder and the servo are mounted on the chassis and are accessible from beneath the car, but they are not well protected from the elements, so they tend to collect a lot of road dirt.

Unusually, the servo can be dismantled for overheaul, and the master-cylinder, too, is designed to be stripped for cleaning and the replacement of seals. Properly maintained, the system is more than capable of coping with the demands of such a fast and heavy car, and a most efficient and easily adjustable handbrake is a further benefit. With both the Mk VIIs I had in regular use I made a point of regularly checking and adjusting the braking system and renewing any parts as necessary, and the result was that I always had powerful brakes that I could depend on in all conditions.

The rear suspension is very straightforward and efficient, the semi-elliptic springs being mounted on strong shackles at their rear end and on the chassis-frame at the front. The springs, which were supplied with protective gaiters, work in unison with lever-type hydraulic shock absorbers, which are mounted on the chassis forward of the axle.

To me, one of the many attractions of the Mk VII was its simple exhaust system, the most expensive part to replace being the front assembly comprising the two downpipes and the flexible joint. The remainder of the system uses pipes with gentle bends and a single silencer, so anyone with welding skills should have little difficulty in fabricating replacement exhaust parts.

At the time I was running Mk VIIs I never came across one with serious rust on the bodywork, but whenever examining one I always made a point of checking the door bottoms and under the rear wheelarches first of all, because these were recognized as common Jaguar weak spots.

The body structure, which incorporates the floorpan, was made from a series of pressings with welded joints, the body then being mounted to the substantial chassis with approximately 24 bolts and screws. The front wings are also bolt-on pressings, so removal and replacement is quite easy apart from the inevitable problem of rusted nuts.

Jaguar must have achieved a higher build quality, or perhaps it was that they were using better-quality steel for the Mk VIIs than on the later Mk VIIIs and IXs, because I never came across bad body rot on cars of up to 15 years of age. But I can recall looking at a five-year-old Mk IX, when it was going for its first MoT test, and despite being undersealed, rot had already taken a serious hold, with both inner sills and the floorpan being so badly corroded that the car was taken off the road because repairs were simply not economical.

However, it looks as though I got off lightly with my Mk VIIs, because talking to current owners not long ago I was surprised to discover just what a problem body rot has since become on these cars. The floor pressings, which consist of the main floor area as well as the raised panel to accommodate the rear seat and the boot floor, can rust quite badly, and from this base the rot can soon spread to the inner wings, the front and centre door pillars and up into the bulkhead. Although I believe that certain repair panels are available, replacement of these areas will still be a complex and very expensive operation, which will probably be beyond the scope of anyone without access to a very spacious workshop with both lifting and welding facilities. Two owners have told me that body removal was necessary in order to carry out welded repairs properly and that the rear inner wings posed a particularly difficult problem. So taking on a rusted Mk VII today could be rather like rebuilding a battleship. Do look very carefully, therefore, before buying, and if possible take along with you someone who has had hands-on experience of this model.

One of the crowning glories of a Mk VII, of course, was its beautiful interior, and I cannot think of any car of its day, regardless of price, which could match its standard of opulence and luxury. But unfortunately, those sumptuous interiors can be extremely costly to renovate, especially as I consider that most work of this type is best left in the hands of a professional; I readily admit that there are only a relatively small number of jobs on a Mk VII interior that I feel comfortable at tackling myself.

It would be wise to think in terms of about £2,000 being gobbled up by renovating or more likely replacing seats, trim and headlining. Good but restorable interiors must be almost impossible to obtain nowadays, yet I can recall buying a full set of seats and trim from a scrapyard for the princely sum of £10. How times change! To most scrap men, anything that could not be cut up and weighed had little value, and bodyshells would be set on fire prior to being cut. But the chance to sell the seats was never passed up because it meant an added cash bonus, although anyone wanting just one seat or a door panel might well have to fork out for the full set, and it's worth remembering that although £10 for a full interior would be laughable today, in 1963 or thereabouts it was quite a tidy sum, enough to buy more than 40 gallons of petrol, and about as much as a young factory worker or a shop worker could expect to earn in a week.

I always made a point of trying to buy any good tyres on wheels from the yards I visited because the 670x16in size were only available from specialist suppliers and were terribly expensive, whereas 50 bob (£2.50) was then an average price of a tyre from a yard. But

When I ran an R-type Bentley for a while, I was always conscious that the Mk VII Jaguar both looked and performed a lot better.

during the late Sixties the supply dried up because a lot of scrap men used Mk VIIIs and IXs for their own transport, often crudely converted to diesel, and so were no longer prepared to sell tyres of this size.

For reasons that I cannot fully understand, Mk VIIs have been something of an ignored model. Perhaps it is because they were thought to be too expensive to maintain, or maybe because they were considered a bit ungainly or insufficiently sporting. In my opinion, nothing could be further from the truth; I have always considered the Mk VII to be a fast sporting saloon (as, of course, its rallying successes proved when it was in its prime), but able to offer luxury and comfort along with its agile performance when driven properly.

At one time, I ran a late-model R-type Bentley with a manual gearbox. The car was in excellent order and I enjoyed owning and driving it, but to me the Mk VII was without doubt the better car in terms of appearance, level of finish of the interior, performance and ease of driving. The relatively cramped interior, long narrow bonnet and heavy steering of the Bentley were a reminder that this was still very much a prewar design, yet when new it would have cost more than a pair of Mk VIIMs. Viewed in that light, the Jaguars were wonderful value.

My last Mk VII came to me entirely by chance. I had been offered a Lagonda by someone who had taken on more cars than he could handle and needed to reduce his assortment. The Lagonda's engine was out and in about a million bits, a lot of parts had been lost and the crank had been damaged beyond repair. I duly bought the car, but in the end I couldn't do anything with it because of the prohibitive cost of spares. But in the corner of the same building I spotted a dusty Mk VIIM. The owner had never got around to doing anything with the car, but it was believed to be in need of a new ring gear. Beneath all the dust lurked a very solid car with an almost new set of tyres, so I paid the asking price for both cars – about £25 for the Lagonda and £35 for the Mk VIIM. I was also able to rescue a Riley 2½-litre roadster, the chassis of which had been earmarked for use as the basis of a stock car until I was able to find a new home for it.

When I set to work on the Mk VIIM, I thought at first that the diagnosis of a broken ring gear was correct because operating the starter produced a loud clatter but it failed to turn the engine. However, the trouble turned out to be a broken starter spring and a couple of damaged flywheel teeth. The teeth were trimmed up with a file, via the starter hole, after which the ring gear served perfectly. So with another starter installed, fresh oil and a new filter, a full service and a minor brake overhaul, the Mk VIIM passed its MoT test.

It was a 1956 model, which had first been registered to a company and later purchased by one of its directors, so there were only two names in the logbook and I was able to confirm that the mileage of around 50,000 was genuine. It was a grey car, with grey interior, and it had been well looked after until its starter broke, after which it had been disposed of and it then stood neglected for a year or so until I came to the rescue. The body and interior responded well to a good clean, both having been the subject of a lot of care in the past, and no other mechanical attention was needed apart from curing a faulty choke unit.

I used this car regularly for about a year, which included some very long journeys, and it never let me down and could still show a remarkable turn of speed. It was a particularly fast Mk VIIM, able to reach at indicated 100mph very quickly, and of course it would cruise happily all day at 80mph on the motorway without any apparent effort. How fortunate were those who were able to use cars like this for their intended purpose – as fast, long-distance tourers on uncluttered continental roads.

Returning home one dark winter evening, I found myself caught behind a convoy of lorries. Then, as we reached a dual carriageway, I pulled out to overtake the vehicles one by one, only to find the drivers bunching up to prevent me from returning to the inside lane. The problem was that some distance away, but coming up fast towards me, were the headlights of something large and heavy. I was doing about 60mph at the time, so the last thing I wanted to do was drop back and be made to look silly, so I quickly dropped down to third, floored the accelerator, whispered 'Come on, old lady!', and flicked the lever back into top as the needle rushed past the three-figure mark. I was through the gap and well clear of the oncoming vehicles before they had become a danger. Not a nice experience, though.

The only reason I eventually parted with the Mk VIIM was that I had simply accumulated too many cars and it just had to go. Someone came a long way by train to view the car, was delighted with it, and it was a strange and rather sad feeling seeing the back of that big grey car as it was driven by someone else to disappear forever after it had given me such good and enjoyable service.

The Mk VII remained in production for about six years, during which more than 30,000 were produced, of which probably about 6,000 were the Mk VIIM version. Yet the cars were never a particularly common sight, probably because most of them enjoyed a relatively short life; not many would have survived more than seven or eight years. As a result, a Mk VII on the road today is a very rare sight, as indeed are most of the other older Jaguars, because all too many of those that remain seem to be kept garaged, or perhaps even stored away, and only brought out onto the road on special occasions. A pity.

The Mk VIII, which replaced the Mk VII, used the same 190bhp engine and basic bodyshell, although it was restyled with a one-piece windscreen, a new grille and frontal treatment, much more chrome trim, cutaway wheel spats and larger rear lights with amber flasher lenses. Somehow, Jaguar had contrived to provide an even more luxurious and stylish interior, with a choice of bench or separate front seats.

The Mk VIII quickly made its predecessor obsolete, although for a time the two models were on sale together, perhaps because there was still a stock of the older car to dispose of and the company wanted to obtain the best possible price for them.

In any case, the Mk VIII would only be in production for a short time, with probably around 6,000 being made in all, before it was succeeded by the Mk IX, a modified and improved version with the 210bhp 3.8-litre engine. It is very difficult to tell the two cars apart at a glance, the rear Mk IX script being the most obvious identity, and a lot of the earlier version retained their value and enjoyed an extended life because they could still be taken for a current model. The Mk IX remained in demand well into the Sixties, enabling more than 10,000 to be built before it gave way to the huge Mk X, which was destined never to sell well.

Although I never owned either model, I did have the pleasure of using a Mk IX for a time. Fitted with a manual gearbox, this stylish car was happy to run from 10 to 110mph in top gear. It was about a couple of years old at the time, and it was an absolute delight to drive. Sadly, though, both models began to rust very quickly, and were doomed in most cases to have an even shorter life than a Mk VII, which means that they, too, are a rare sight on the roads today.

All three models, Mk VII, VIII and IX, just oozed style, but the Mk IX in particular was a car that looked good anywhere. The example I have seen most recently was on display at an all-makes rally, and of all the cars present this was the one which attracted the most attention. But, perhaps out of sentiment, the Mk VIIM has a special place in my memory bank. It had something in its styling that somehow the later cars were unable quite to capture, and I am still convinced that they were more solidly built.

CHAPTER 4

Mk Is and Mk IIs

"It is sad that so many Mk IIs were neglected from such an early age and then bodged from then on."

It was inevitable that sooner or later Jaguar would be making cars of monocoque construction, rather than with a separate chassis and body, and of course the big day arrived in 1955 with the unveiling of the all-new Jaguar 2.4. It was destined to be the first of a long line of compact models, which served instantly to broaden Jaguar's customer base, for not everyone needed, or indeed could afford, the big Mk VII saloons or their direct successors.

Although later models with larger engines were to prove more popular in the long run, there is no doubt that the 2.4 was the right car, at the right price, at the time of its launch, and it attracted a lot of buyers who, because the Mk VII was too large for them, had been forced to look at other makes – typically Humber, Sunbeam, Riley, Rover, or perhaps Armstrong Siddeley with their 234 saloon – for a suitably sized and priced car.

My first 2.4 was a 1959 Mk I model and it was already five years old by the time I bought it, so quite a lot had happened within the compact Jaguar range by that time. The engine of the 2.4 was a shorter-stroke version of the 3.4-litre XK unit, and it used twin Solex carburettors with a manual choke, giving it a healthy 112bhp, good fuel consumption and a top speed of over 100mph.

Completely different from that of other Jaguars, the front suspension of wishbones, coil springs and telescopic dampers was mounted on a separate pressed-steel subframe, which also served as the front engine mounting and was fixed to the body underframe with Metalastic blocks, which ensured good insulation from road shocks and provided a very smooth ride.

Steering was by a conventional recirculating-ball box and idler assembly, also bolted to the front subframe, the steering column being split by rubber-mounted joints to enable the front assembly to be easily separated from the column. But right from the car's introduction there were complaints about the steering being too low-geared as well as heavy, a criticism that would remain with the car and with the subsequent Mk II versions.

The rear suspension, unique to this model, employed long cantilever springs, the rear of which were fixed to the axle through rubber-bonded bushes. The centre part of the springs was mounted at the rear of the 'top hat' section to the main chassis rails, being held in place between two plates with rubber mounts, while the front of the springs was secured by rubber pads. A pair of forward-facing torque arms secured the axle to a crossmember running under the rear seat area. Side location was by means of a Panhard rod, and telescopic dampers were used.

Early cars were plagued by rear suspension problems and rear-end noise, clunks and heavy rattles from the springs and mountings being the most common faults. But far more seriously on early cars, the mountings for the Panhard rod could break away under load and put the driver into a frightening and potentially dangerous situation; anyone who has tried to control one of these cars when the Panhard rod has been simply out of alignment will

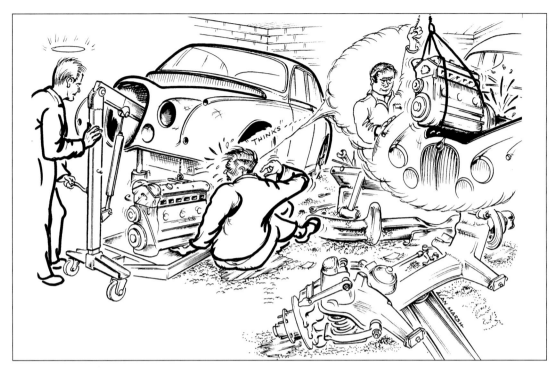

I have seen far too many people suffer trapped fingers through attempting to lift an engine where there is insufficient space to tackle the job properly.

understand the predicament in the event of a complete breakage. The fact that the rear track of what subsequently became known as a Mk I was considerably narrower than the front served to further underline the cars' early reputation for unpredictable cornering behaviour.

Most 2.4s were fitted with the Moss four-speed manual gearbox as used in the Mk VII, and although an automatic gearbox became available on later cars, so much of the available power was absorbed by the torque converter that few automatic 2.4s were produced and even fewer survived.

As with the earlier 1½-litre cars, Jaguar's policy was to keep the price as low as possible to encourage sales, and to this end they used many parts from other cars in the range. This keen pricing strategy was to pay considerable dividends, and during its four years in production around 20,000 Mk I 2.4s would be sold worldwide.

Early in 1957 it was joined by the 3.4, which used the same bodyshell, but was instantly recognizable by its cutaway rear wheel covers, a wider grille and twin exhaust pipes. The 3.4's engine was as fitted to the XK140, and with twin SU carburettors it developed 210bhp, making it the first true 120mph Jaguar saloon. There was a choice of a four-speed manual gearbox or automatic transmission, but surprisingly the car came on to the market with drum brakes, which proved hopelessly inadequate for a car of the 3.4's performance; as Dunlop discs were made an option almost straight away, very few cars were to be sold with drum brakes. The early discs as fitted to both sizes of Mk I had round pads, and to change them meant removing the calipers. This, of course, meant that it was necessary to bleed the system, which made it an expensive and lengthy operation. Later cars had modified brakes with square, quick-change pads.

Sadly, the Mk Is, with their narrow rear ends and small windows, quickly became dated, and from the early Sixties they became just another obsolete car as prices plummeted, and those who might have gone for one secondhand preferred to wait until they could afford a Mk II, which was still a current model. Quite suddenly, Mk Is were littering the scrapyards, many of them ending their lives there because repairs were becoming uneconomical; many owners begrudged having to pay for new tyres or brake parts, while the cost of a clutch or an exhaust system was probably as much as was needed for a deposit on a new car. Yet I loved the elegant and sporting lines of the Mk I, especially the later version with its cutaway spats and wider grille; to me, it had an appeal that the Mk II was never quite able to match.

My first Mk I, finished in Pearl Grey with a red interior, had been well looked after by its one previous owner and it came my way because faults had developed in the automatic gearbox. The quote for putting these right was so astronomical that the owner decided to buy a Mk II instead. I cannot remember how much it cost me, but it couldn't be much because I recall that no-one else was prepared to take on the liability of sorting out the transmission.

This was the first conversion I did from an automatic to a manual gearbox, but I was committed to it because in the first place I loathed automatics, and secondly, I felt that a Jaguar was never the same without a gearbox you could stir. Although the work proved time-consuming and heavy, it was not particularly difficult, and of course in the days when parts could be picked up so cheaply from the scrapyards, the cost was not excessive; I dread to think what it would be today for such a large shopping list. In the end, I needed the manual gearbox, a flywheel and clutch assembly, clutch slave cylinder, gearbox crossmember, propshaft, starter motor, brake and clutch pedal assembly, as well as replacement front seats and interior trim. The automatic Mk Is were supplied with a split bench front seat, which I decided to replace with the preferred bucket-type seats in the correct colour, while the dashboard-mounted gear selector had to be removed and a suitable piece of dash trim inserted in its place.

Although I would recommend anyone undertaking work on a Jaguar to acquire the best available workshop manual for the model in question, and follow the advice offered, I have to admit that I always employed my own method of removing the engine and gearbox from compact saloons, whilst accepting that I was most fortunate in having available the proper facilities for doing so.

I would remove the engine and gearbox, as a single unit, through the engine bay, which calls for a high roof and a strong pulley block. It makes life easier if the car can be placed over a pit as this allows the tail end of the gearbox to be manoeuvred and the unit then to be lifted vertically and swiftly clear of the car. This is the easiest and most efficient method I know, but it is as well to remember that Jaguar engines are extremely heavy, so my advice to anyone who lacks the proper equipment is simply not to even think about tackling it. I have seen far too many people suffer trapped fingers through attempting to lift an engine where there is insufficient space to tackle the job properly.

My conversion turned out well, in fact the trickiest bits proved to be cutting the correct size of hole for the gear-lever, fitting pieces of carpet accurately and filling in the space on the dash where the gear selector had been. Apart from routine servicing, the car required no work on it, because it was completely rot-free and I made sure I kept it that way.

From the time I first acquired a compressor, I sprayed the underside of all my cars with oil, also the box sections and anywhere else within reach, using one of the underbody seal-type sprayguns and an old container. This is a very worthwhile job, but do make sure that you let your car drip somewhere harmlessly before you park it in your driveway!

This proved to be one of the most appealing Jaguars I have owned. It performed very well and always seemed to go a long way on a tankful of fuel. Although I had changed it to manual transmission, I retained the original back axle, as I did with subsequent conversions of this sort, because it didn't seem to do anything to reduce the performance. Then one day I attended a vintage car rally, and when I returned to the car park I found a chap drooling over the little grey Jag. He pestered me for weeks until he eventually persuaded me to sell it to him. He only ever used it for pleasure motoring, but I was glad that I had passed it on to an appreciative new owner.

Of course, the earliest Mk Is are now more than 40 years old, while the last of the Mk IIs left the factory more than 25 years ago, so since then there cannot have been many of the compact saloons to have escaped being bodged up in one form or another, and some of them will have undergone this indignity several times, quite likely without the knowledge of their current owners. With the over-inflated prices which have prevailed in recent years, the temptation to cover up the sins of deterioration have had a particularly strong financial attraction to the unscrupulous, but the phenomenon is a far from new one, and I can recall seeing cars – perhaps Mk IIs more than Mk Is – which were only two or three years old and had already had appalling things done to them so that they could be tarted up to lure an eager buyer.

The Mk I on which I did the most extensive work had been treated in such a manner. It was a late 3.4 and had been bought by a friend of mine from a large and supposedly reputable dealer. It turned out to be the first compact Jaguar saloon I saw suffering from really serious corrosion. The unhappy owner of this monstrosity thought he was quite capable of appraising a car, but his problem was that he was an honest man and so he had expected those with whom he did business to behave in a similar manner.

The red 3.4 had a black interior and wire wheels, which was exactly as it had been turned out at the factory. But the fact that its first owner had been running a plant hire company and had put up a high mileage touring building sites had been cleverly disguised by the surreptitious application for a duplicate logbook. Up on a ramp, the car looked fine – nice and clean, always undersealed, they said. The paintwork was good, too, and the interior likewise, everything seemed to work, it drove well, and apparently it had had quite a lot of replacement bits, including a new clutch. At this time, clean, well-equipped Mk I 3.4s were still commanding quite a high price, and this one certainly wasn't cheap, but my friend liked it and decided to buy it.

The first problem was a corroded petrol tank. It was quite a common fault on these models, but this one was so rotten that the bottom fell out. It had been badly repaired with

I would always spray the underside of my cars with oil . . . but if you do this, be sure to let your car drip somewhere harmlessly before you park it on the driveway!

meat safe gauze and body filler and then covered with underseal. When confronted with the evidence the supplier of the car was less than sympathetic, and so although I was not in the habit of doing other people's repairs, in this instance I obtained a good secondhand tank and agreed to fit it, which was when the other problems began to be revealed.

Removal of the tank exposed extensive and badly repaired rot on the rear wing, below the filler cap. With the car hoisted high on stands, the new owner and I were able to take a much closer look at the underside, and it was immediately apparent that new sills had been fitted, but had only been tacked on, while the inner seals seemed to be made from some sort of plastic.

We removed a sill to find that our worst fears were confirmed. Just enough of the inner sill remained for the new sill to be welded on with the aid of a few tacks, the gap where the metal inner sill should have been being filled with what looked to be about half a ton of body filler. The outer sills on the compact saloons are not structural, but the inners most certainly are, and this car was in need of some extensive and costly welding.

The thick underseal on the floorpan covered a layer of rust – almost certainly a legacy of the first owner's frequent visits to building sites – and coatings of wet cement, mortar, etc had quickly caused corrosion. Furthermore, the job of fitting a replacement clutch had been carried out the easy way – by cutting holes through the metal floor from the inside in order to gain access to the bolts which, when undone, enabled the 'box to be removed from underneath. An RAC engineer was brought in to do a full inspection at my garage, after which it became a legal battle between the garage which had sold the car and my friend's solicitors, who in the end were able to get him his money back. But the sad part about it all was that all that deterioration had taken place on a car which was still only three or four years old.

Although a lot of drivers were just a little intimidated by the Mk I on corners, perhaps mindful that Mike Hawthorn had come to grief in one of them, I have to admit that I enjoyed the way they handled and quickly learned how to take them briskly yet tidily through a corner. But there was certainly a knack to it, and that narrow tail could bite back quite nastily if you didn't treat it with respect.

I bought what turned out to be both my last and my favourite Mk I quite by chance at an auction. Although I had never been a great supporter of auctions, I agreed to go along to this one because a friend was keen for me to examine a Bentley Mk 6 he was interested in bidding for. Having done so, I noticed this Cotswold Blue Mk I and just had time to feel under the sills and inners and to check the rear spring hangers before the bidding began. The engine was missing quite badly, but otherwise sounded OK, the car had a long MoT certificate and in due course it became mine for £36, which was a very fair price in 1969.

I began to drive it home behind my friend's Bentley, which had cost him just a few pounds more, but soon I was wishing I hadn't bothered. The Jaguar began to splutter, backfire and boil over, and one backfire was so violent it almost took the ends off the silencers. I just managed to get it home and dumped it outside the workshop doors, where it stood for several days because I fully intended to admit my mistake and send it for scrap.

But fortunately, a visiting pal took an interest in the car, and when probing around under the bonnet he discovered that some comic had switched the plug leads round in the distributor cap. Once the leads had been sorted out the engine ran like a dream, in fact the last XK engine I had heard sounding as sweet as this one was in the paddock at Oulton Park, so I immediately began to take a greater interest in my new Jaguar, which clearly had not been on the road for some time.

It soon became apparent, too, that this was not exactly an ordinary 3.4, but was one that had been 'breathed upon'. First of all there was the 140mph speedometer, then there was the gearbox, which felt a little more precise and easier to work than the usual one. There was nothing very special under the bonnet except that the carbs somehow looked just a touch larger, but the slightest touch on the accelerator pedal was enough to send the rev-counter

It can take two to untangle a cylinder head from the block, and a rubber-headed 'persuader' close to hand can sometimes provide useful extra assistance.

needle spinning round the dial. This without doubt turned out to be one of the fastest Jaguars I have ever owned or driven, with acceleration far quicker than any 3.8 that came my way, and which on one memorable occasion actually saw off a 4.2 E-type whose owner tried to out-run me on a motorway!

I never did find out what its true top speed was, but I once had a big burst with it and saw the speedo needle get to the end of the dial, so that was probably on the far side of 130mph. But I think the car's main fascination for me from the performance standpoint was its ability to rush up hills; most Jaguars are pretty good hill-climbers, but this one really excelled.

Close to home, part of the main road consisted of a straight but steep climb about half a mile long, and in the late Sixties few cars, even with a good run at it, could climb it in top gear, and most ran out of power even in third. One Sunday morning I set off with a friend to buy some papers and cigarettes and stopped almost immediately to give two neighbours a lift. Both of them were big chaps, well over 15 stone, so I had plenty of weight on board when I got to the end of the minor road which joined the main road at the bottom of the hill.

One of the passengers, who had previously owned an XK, asked what the 3.4 was like climbing hills, so I decided to show him. I turned into the main road, then parked and waited for the light traffic to clear before setting off from a standing start. About halfway up we went past a railway station and a church on our right at about 70mph in top, to the considerable surprise of the churchgoers as the wonderful sound of the exhaust bounced off the stone wall on our left, and we continued on up until we went over the brow of the hill, still accelerating, at 85mph, to the amazement of my highly impressed passengers. It may sound a tall story, but I have three witnesses to vouch for its truth! That car stayed with me for a considerable time, but like so many others it eventually found an appreciative new owner.

I have already indicated that these compact Jaguars are no strangers to corrosion, so careful and comprehensive inspection is vital if heartache and disappointment are to be avoided. For example, fuel tanks have always been a problem on these cars. Due to their location they get a lot of road dirt thrown at them and packs of mud can quickly accumulate between the tank and the body. The trouble usually starts with pinholes, often near the joint along the bottom, but once the rust takes hold it quickly spreads.

I have successfully carried out repairs to these tanks with the aid of matting and resin, using special fire-resistant materials (not glassfibre, as used for body repairs), and if care is taken and the rust holes are not too big, a repair of this type will last for years. I have also used similar techniques for reinforcing tanks before they have started to rust.

Always remove the tank, rub down the rust by hand, using either production paper or coarse wet and dry, and of course don't even think about using power tools, which can cause sparks, with devastating results. Treat the rust with an inhibitor, then build up a coating of resin and matting. I used to get the best results with the fine tissue, but this was purely a personal preference. Be prepared to spend several days over the job to ensure that you end up with a good coating all around the bottom edge of the tank. I would coat the tank with matting up to about the halfway point, then paint the entire tank with resin, which proved to be an excellent rust treatment. Finally, finish off with underseal, a bitumin-based paint, or whatever you prefer. Because new tanks were very expensive, I treated the tanks of many cars in this way.

The compact saloons also have a brake vacuum storage tank located under the front wing, and if this tank is holed one of the first signs will be a very heavy brake pedal and a reluctance for the car to stop! A common but dangerous dodge at one time was to replace a rusted tank with a similar looking but much lighter one as used in the wiper system of a Ford 100E. Some people even went to the trouble of getting these tanks from scrapyards and adapting them to fit, which apart from anything else seemed an awful lot of trouble to go to bearing in mind that the air tanks only cost about £5 new. My Mk I had been bodged with one of these tanks, which I speedily replaced with a proper one, and at the same time I welded in a new front crossmember and angle pieces, which are not structural, but help to support the front wing assembly. These would wear very thin on some cars, yet on others they would last for years. I was fortunate in being able to have these sections made in galvanized material, which I could then cut to the required size before welding in.

An unusual feature of this Mk I was its rear light assembly. Very early in its life, combined red and amber units, similar to those used on Mk IIs, had been fitted and they matched the body contour perfectly. Yet as far as I am aware neither the Mk II's nor the XK's lamp units would fit these cars and I have never seen another Mk I with them fitted. It was all a bit of a mystery, but I thought they suited the car and they certainly gave a better warning to following drivers.

The Mk II Jaguars had been introduced in late 1959 in three engine sizes – 2.4, 3.4 and 3.8 litres. Outwardly, the cars were almost identical, although as with the Mk I the 2.4-litre version was identifiable by its single exhaust pipe. The most important changes to the new car were its wider rear track, improved visibility as a result of the increase in glass area and the completely new interior. They were an instant success, and during a production run of roughly eight years around 25,000 2.4s, almost 30,000 3.4s and more than that number of 3.8s were produced. Later, of course, came the 240 and 340 models which, though much maligned at the time, in reality gave both better performance and improved economy over the Mk IIs they replaced. All these compact Jaguars had many mechanical and body similarities, and therefore tended to suffer from the same faults, so the majority of the guidelines I offer later in this chapter should be equally valid for, say, a 1956 2.4 as for a 1969 340.

I only had one 2.4 Mk II, and frankly I was very disappointed with it, despite some quite extensive modifications in an effort to improve its performance. Even though it had more power than its predecessor, this model proved to be something of a sluggard, and even when fully run in it would never reach 100mph, and in consequence was never made available for road testing by the press. The 3.4 was just a little slower than its Mk I equivalent, but of course with its wider rear track it handled a lot better, while as expected the 3.8 could out-accelerate the 3.4, although the top speed of the two cars was very similar. My personal favourite was the 3.4, mainly because of its sweeter engine, but also because it was less prone to oil problems than the 3.8.

I bought my 2.4 because at that time I was doing a lot of short journeys in heavy traffic and I thought the low fuel consumption would be an advantage. At first, it was so slow – even compared with my old Mk I – that I thought there was something wrong with the car, so I asked a local garage owner to give it a run. He came back puzzled, saying that he thought it went well for a 2.4. So one weekend I fitted another head and cams, together with a pair of SUs, not that it made a lot of difference. It would just about stagger up to 100mph on the motorway, but economy was now not much better than the bigger car's, and the final insult came when a Ford Zephyr Mk IV passed me on a hill. Yet funnily enough, the chap to whom I eventually sold the car loved it. I saw it every day for years afterwards and it gave him at least 10 years of very happy motoring.

It is sad that so many Mk IIs were neglected from such an early age and then bodged from then on. The reason for this is that many of them were first bought as company cars, but then were sold on to private owners after a couple of years, many of whom either could not afford or simply begrudged the considerable cost involved in having their car properly maintained. Jaguar parts have always been relatively expensive, and few owners of Mk IIs were interested in doing their own repairs; a Jag was something to drive rather than crawl under, and by about 1963 the auctions were full of cheap Mk IIs, most of them ending up

Beware, XK cylinder heads are not exactly lightweights . . . !

with dealers who were skilled in the art of covering up their faults. Then, with gleaming paint and interior, boot-blacked tyres and a dubious MoT certificate, these tired yet still current models would quickly find new and unsuspecting owners.

My first Mk II was a 3.4 bought from someone who regretted ever setting eyes on it. It was certainly not short of problems, but most of them I was able to put right quite quickly, whereas for someone at the mercy of a garage or bodyshop the cost would have been horrific. It was a 1960 car in British Racing Green with a green interior and wire wheels. It must have done about 10,000 miles since its last oil and filter change, the top chain was rattling badly and the camshaft on one side sounded as if it was about to disintegrate.

As usual, the handbrake was useless and the footbrake was not much better, but basically the engine seemed sound, with good oil pressure, and the clutch was OK. The body also seemed solid enough, as did the underside, just a few small rust patches along the bottom of the sills – not a big job there, I thought.

Removing and working on an XK overhead-camshaft cylinder head never held any terrors for me, but the heads are quite heavy, so a little help is always useful, but first, always read the manual, if there is one, and be prepared to obey it. One of the most important things to remember is to place the head on the bench in such a way as not to damage the valves. Also, never try to turn the cams before reading the section on how to work on the head. The proper way is first to remove the cam that is not being worked on, thus enabling the other cam to be revolved to check clearances, etc, without bending the valves. Each camshaft should only be replaced after lining it up, using the special camshaft tool. The head is always removed or replaced with the cams in such a position.

One of the most laborious jobs when working on the valves is setting the valve clearances,

Getting those sills to fit was something of a nightmare . . .

Bliss! Getting behind the wheel of a Jaguar after restoring it to good health has always been one of the great joys in my life.

which is done by means of interchangeable shims, which are supposed to be marked by thickness. This is a long, slow job, but it must be done correctly because once the head is on it's too late to do anything about it. I was fortunate in obtaining a load of these shims from a friendly garage, and I freely admit that I couldn't have completed the job without such a good selection. A tip I heard was to coat cam, follower and shim with clean oil, thus ensuring that the clearance would remain the same when the car was running and that the engine was suitably quiet; I always insist that there should be no noise from properly set up cams. In the course of working on this engine I fitted two good secondhand cams and a new top chain and tensioner, after which it ran very well and never gave a hint of trouble.

The heater, however, was a problem I never managed to overcome. Never a strong point on Jaguars, this one made up its own mind whether to blow hot or cold air, and in the end I gave up with it. The poor braking was caused simply through neglect, some of the calipers being partly seized, but penetrating oil and new pads put that matter right. The handbrakes on Mk I and Mk II Jaguars are adequate if properly maintained, the most common problem being the caliper seizing on its fulcrum bolt, but if the pads are not worn down too far and the cables are correctly adjusted the handbrake will do its job.

This was one of the few Mk IIs I owned which had new Panhard rod rubbers fitted properly and the rod set at the correct length – an easy enough job to do, yet so often done wrongly and as a result having such a strange effect on the steering.

A few weeks after I bought the car I decided to fit new sills, a job I had not tackled before. One tip I learnt a long time ago is never to remove a body panel until you have the new one ready to fit; half an inch too much metal cut out in the wrong place is not always easy to put back!

So, with the 3.4 resting high on four stands, the old sills came off, which proved to be quite a complicated and dirty job. It meant removing all the tread plates in order to cut the top of the sills away, and the most difficult task was removing the bit of sill that tucks behind the front wing. I remember using proper original equipment parts, which were expensive, but they were still difficult to fit because at the factory the sills must have been fitted before the wings.

With the sills cut off I came across a problem I was to see many more times on Mk IIs; the sills had rusted badly from the inside. Even though the surface was now quite dry, it appeared that at some time the sills had been full of water, hence the rust. Pleased that I had not delayed the job any longer, I was able to repair the inners and coat them with an effective rust treatment. I also made holes of about a quarter-inch diameter at the front and back of the underside of each sill, and when the job was completed I filled the sills with oil via a hole in the top. Then, over a period of several days, I left the car parked, first nose-up, then nose-down, until the excess had drained out.

Getting those sills to fit was something of a nightmare, as it can be with most Jaguar panels. It is a case of getting an initial fit, checking the gaps, then using a pop rivet or a self-tapper, checking again, then applying the first tacks of weld, by gas, of course.

Incidentally, welding of any sort is something I would never think about doing without a firewatcher and at least a bucket of water and a sponge handy. There is sealant, padding, insulation and trim everywhere, and wires passing through sills and box sections which need special care. So never work alone; you could easily melt or damage a piece of trim, and remember that that piece of smouldering felt could all too quickly become a major fire.

In due course my BRG 3.4 made way in a straight swap for a later 3.8 in a metallic blue with beige trim. It had belonged to a good friend, who had always liked the car, but was completely honest about the fact that it had consumed petrol at a frightening rate. Fortunately, a carb overhaul and some attention to the automatic choke, followed by a professional tune-up, did wonders for the fuel bills and so I decided to run this car for a while. It certainly ran well, and its acceleration was much better than the 3.4's.

Apart from some minor work on the brakes, it seemed that little else needed doing, but unfortunately I soon discovered that this car consumed oil at an alarming rate. Quite a lot of it dripped away from various points whenever it was parked and I can only think that the rest disappeared during use because it was not an oil burner in the conventional sense due to engine wear. Other 3.8 owners confirmed to me that this was not uncommon, and after I discovered that during a journey of about 200 miles to London I had used about a gallon of oil I decided that perhaps it was time to let the car go.

Despite this experience, I did have another 3.8 for a short time, a very clean 1963 car in light maroon metallic with chromed wire wheels and a most opulent interior trimmed in off-white hide, but it soon became clear that the car had been badly treated and the gearbox needed changing. As Mk IIs were almost worthless at the time, I never got round to changing the 'box and the car eventually went for scrap.

During the late Sixties and early Seventies £50 would have bought a tidy Mk II and well worn and rather tatty examples stood on many a car lot at around £35 each. I think at that time I must have been the only person in the world to have any interest in them, but I liked them and used them regularly well into the Seventies, undertaking quite a costly major rebuild on one car which other people had dismissed as being a waste of money. In purely financial terms, of course, they were right, but I decided it was a small enough price to pay for the enjoyment the car would bring me.

The main donor car for this project was an early 3.4 in Sherwood Green with a completely rust-free underside. In fact, apart from some bubbling on the front wings there was no sign of rot whatsoever. First of all I stripped the car down to the bare shell, the only things left in place being the wiring, the dashboard and the headlining, plus the doors, but these were stripped of all trim and fittings. Then, with the aid of a roll-over frame, I stripped the underside back to the bare metal, which confirmed the lack of rust, but both sills had been scraped and badly repaired, so I decided to replace them.

After fitting the sills, I treated the underside with rust inhibitor and several coats of zinc-rich paint, then came the job of fitting a pair of new front wings, which was something I was not looking forward to. I ordered the wings from a main agent in north Lancashire (I think they cost about £38 each) and they were despatched to me the same day via British Rail, Red Star express. A week later there was still no sign of the wings, but the suppliers were very good about it, putting in an insurance claim and managing to find me another pair, which this time I picked up and brought back by road.

Years later I was still having nightmares about getting those wings to fit! I had waited until the engine was back in place, clearance being so critical. Every gap must be perfect, especially the gap between wheelarch and wheel, otherwise the wheel will foul the wing. It was ages before I dared make a weld, but in the end it all went together properly, someone leaded the joints for me, and when it came to fitting the grille it lined up perfectly. Relief!

For the respray, in British Racing Green, I used an acrylic for the first time and found it a pleasure to work with, but like so many of those paints it looked such an obvious respray at first. However, a week or so of weathering caused it to settle back, after which it looked wonderful.

The chance to acquire a new but 'shop soiled' 3.4 block and a balanced crank was an opportunity not to be missed, and I used conrods from another engine with new bushes, etc, new 9:1 pistons, bearings, chains, etc, and a reconditioned and balanced flywheel with new clutch parts. The head was a rebuilt C-spec unit with matched cams and rebuilt 2in SU carburettors together with a standard exhaust system.

As a change from the old-type gearbox I fitted a modern all-synchro unit, and at the back I had a Powerlok differential. The front suspension was overhauled, as was the complete braking system, including new copper pipes all round, and the car's wire wheels were stove enamelled and fitted with a set of new radials to finish the job off nicely.

The immaculate red interior came from another car and after being cleaned it looked like new. The original headlining was retained, as was the dash and all the woodwork, which I had repolished. The result, after many hours of enjoyable but hard work, was a very pleasing car, which looked like a well-kept year old one. This was exactly what I had wanted to achieve, rather than an obvious re-creation.

Retaining its original registration number, the car became a crowd-puller whenever it was parked. It also performed very well, with rapid acceleration and a top speed of over 125mph. I was happy to drive that car at high speed under most conditions because it was a joy to handle, and it was also one of the most economical 3.4s I have ever owned.

I kept it for about a year after the rebuild, and then, just before I parted with it, I received a postcard from British Rail telling me that a parcel for me was awaiting collection at Manchester station. Expecting some conifer trees my wife had ordered some weeks earlier, I was amazed to find instead a pair of somewhat scratched Jaguar wings!

As you will probably have gathered by now, I greatly enjoyed my experiences with Mk Is and Mk IIs – working on them, driving them and even just owning them. They're still stylish and attractive cars today, and the bigger-engined ones can certainly hold their own on modern congested roads. So they are still a practical car to own, capable of being looked after by an enthusiastic owner, only the sheer weight of some of the components putting a few tasks beyond the reach of DIY people.

But sadly, the bodgers are still handling Mk IIs, which perhaps is not surprising bearing in mind the prices they have been commanding, and many of the despicable tricks of the Sixties are still being performed on these cars. A nice coat of paint can be dangerously deceiving, deflecting the eye from more serious things, and a bad compact Jaguar can be not only a danger to use, but an endless drain on finances.

My advice to anyone contemplating the purchase of one of these cars, therefore, is do not hesitate to seek advice from an experienced owner, preferably one who is a member of one of the Jaguar clubs. Don't go alone to look at a car – a second opinion is always worthwhile –

and beware of dealers and other vendors who have poor facilities for inspection. Finally, beware of 'basket cases' in the guise of rust-free US imports. Most of the good ex-US cars were snapped up years ago, and in recent times the contents of entire scrapyards have been shipped over here. Should you ever see one of the legendary Coombs-converted cars on sale, be very wary. Only about 28 of them were ever produced, and despite the legends they were not all red with louvred bonnets. I am in no sense an expert on these cars, but I understand that the best source of information on them is the Jaguar Enthusiasts Club.

The main concern of anyone seeking a compact Jaguar saloon should be the state of the bodyshell. Like the other mass-produced cars of the time, they had to be built to a price, and not a lot of attention was given to the prevention of rust. These cars have mud and water traps aplenty, and the rust process started very early in their lives, so it must be impossible now to find one in its original state without some degree of welded repair or panel replacement.

If this work has been done properly, fine, because such things are part of a car's history, can add to its interest and, most important, can give the new owner peace of mind. So start by looking at all the gaps. The first thing I would look for would be a nice even space between the door bottom and the sill, then I would check the vertical gaps between door and front wing and between the doors. Badly spaced doors not only look unsightly on these cars, they are also a sign of badly fitted replacement panels or accident repairs.

Use your discretion. It may be, for example, that a car has been fitted with a set of good secondhand doors, or perhaps even had some repair panels on the front wings. Look along the body sides for signs of uneven panels or ripples; on the Mk II in particular the door panels could rust from the inside due to water being trapped by the felt insulation. Also, test the panels for the presence of filler. Body filler is a quite acceptable material when used for its proper purpose, which is to prepare an uneven surface, most often a welded area, prior to painting. Used in moderation, plastic fillers are fine, but thick layers of the stuff are not and can usually be detected by tapping a panel gently – a dull thud usually gives the game away.

Look carefully at the door frames, in particular the bottoms, which are always among the first places to rust. Are they still solid original metal, or have they been repaired, and if so, how well? Possibly the car has had new door skins fitted, which is perfectly acceptable if the job has been done correctly, but the bent-over lip will often be a giveaway in such a case because it is unlikely to be as neat as the factory machine-pressed joint.

The low-mounted outer sills of these cars are very susceptible to damage from kerbs, so light filling is acceptable, although I must say that I always prefer to see new sills to repaired ones. Also, be very cautious if new panels have been fitted on top of rusty old ones, allowing the old ones to fester away underneath. At one time this was a very common dodge as it saved the operator a lot of preparation time; quite often the rusty originals were flattened with a hammer to enable the replacements to fit closely. This can be quite difficult to spot, just about the only giveaway being the top joint near to the tread plates. Look for welding at the point where the sill joins the door aperture; a properly fitted sill should be joined at the inner edge of the door aperture, the doorstep being part of the sill. But this is not always the case, and many people who fit sills in the most thorough way prefer to make a welded joint, leaving the original doorsteps in place. Some good quality sills have been produced in that style. Properly fitted sills should tuck behind the front wing and the joint between the two panels filled. Correctly made, this joint should neither flex nor crack, which means that should it do either, it is probably an indication of cover-up sills.

Some cars may have had their jacking points removed altogether. These were partly supported by the original sill, which was a poor design feature because it was quite common to see cars only a couple of years old with a crumpled sill and jacking point. A proper repair in this case would involve extensive welding, so I see no objection to them being carefully removed. I would never have considered using the original jacking point on a compact saloon in any case, always preferring to use a sturdy scissors-type jack which could be

Pay attention to the entire floorpan in search of disguised rust and repairs, and remember that the inner sills should be solid metal.

pushed under the front or rear suspension when the need arose.

Another rust trap is on what is best termed the lower rear wing, being the bit behind the wheelarch which is partly concealed by the bumper. Both sides of the car, but in particular the side housing the fuel tank, become packed with mud, and badly carried out repairs are common in these areas, despite the fact that repair panels are now available. Look upwards from the underside for patched joints, although these may well be heavily disguised with underseal, and look at the bottom edge for filler, remembering that the original panels had a tidy, right-angled edge. Two of the rear bumper mounts are fixed to these side panels, and traces of welding burn or body filler on the rubber bumper mounts are often a clue to dodgy repairs. Also, look carefully at the rear valance, which is partly hidden by the bumper, as often this will be sound on the outside, but rusted inside. Before leaving the back of the car, check the fuel tank for leaks or cheap repairs; body fillers and various forms of plastic metal are used.

Moving to the front, start by checking the wheelarches, which should have a clean and fairly sharp edge, so any signs of body filler should be easy to spot. The rearmost part, between the wheelarch and the door, deserves special attention as this larger area can rust badly, especially at the bottom, near the sill. Repairs in this area using tin sheets, or even bits of cardboard or plastic, are not uncommon, even though proper repair pieces are made for this and other parts of the front wings.

On Mk IIs, look for rust around the sidelight mounting, and on both these and Mk Is in the area of the front flasher/sidelight units, while another bad spot is the front bottom edge of the wings, which is partly hidden by the front bumper. This front valance, which dips and joins in the centre, was always quick to rust, and as it is part of the main wing pressing any rust starting here is quick to spread to the main wing area.

All the chromium-plated parts on these cars are expensive to replace and the parts made from cast mazak should be looked at very carefully as complete replacement is the only solution to pitted chrome. Reproduction castings are on the market, but are certainly not cheap. Bumpers, overriders and possibly grilles can be replated, but be prepared to be shocked when asking for prices.

If possible, inspect the car on a ramp, or if not, then jack the front up as high as possible, put it on to secure stands and then crawl underneath, repeating the process to look at the rear end. Starting behind the front bumper, examine the crossmember and its two angle pieces, which are made of light channel section, this formation being joined on either side to the front wing lower valance, on the outer curve, by small pierced panels known as crow's feet. Although the whole structure, which is there mainly to steady the front wings, rusts easily, it is easily replaced at a reasonable cost.

Pay attention to the entire floorpan in search of disguised rust and repairs, and remember that the inner sills should be solid metal. Next, examine the main chassis rails; as the front ends are often coated in engine oil they tend to be quite solid. The rear of these rails forms the support for the back springs, which sit in a box section, the springs being held between stout rubber blocks and kept secure with metal plates fixed to the box section by four bolts. This assembly is clearly visible from beneath the car, so ensure that all the metal in this area is sound and that the inner section of the box, which keeps the springs away from the body, is still in place. It is common – and quite acceptable – to find extensive welded repairs in this area, just so long as the job has been done properly.

The Panhard rod mounting should also be sound and firm, as must be the metal surrounding it, the area at the front inner edge of the offside wheelarch; again, welded repairs can be expected here. Look closely at the mounting for the torque arms, which takes the form of a crossmember running at the back of the rear seat pressing. This rear seat pan, along with the wheelarches, should be sound, so look for rust around the edges where the panels meet as this whole rear area is an important part of the structure. In looking as closely as possible up under the wheelarches and in the area of the rear valance and wheel tray, be wary of any patches of thick underseal. If possible, try to look under the rear seat squab for rust or repairs as the wheelarches here are covered in vinyl, which can hide all sorts of horrors, crude glassfibre repairs being quite common under the covering. Also, have a good look inside the boot, in particular around the shock absorber mounts and where the wheelarch joins the boot floor.

Finally, after deciding that any structural faults can be repaired, or tolerated short-term, there is one more important point to check, and as far as I am concerned this single fact would be reason enough for deciding not to buy. Difficult as it may be to do so, somehow you must make certain that the metal gearbox cowling, which is part of the main structure, has never been cut. To enable the gearbox to be removed from under the car, many dodgy repairers cut around the bulkhead area, often taking large pieces out in order to get at those bellhousing bolts to which I referred earlier. Even if the metal has been welded up again, which is very unlikely, my advice would be to leave the car where it is and buy another one. My main aversion to such methods is not the weakening of the structure, but the fact that any car butchered in this manner is likely to have had other 'short cut' jobs performed on it during its life.

Jaguar interiors are expensive to work on, although with the range of products on the market today there is much the owner can do to improve a grubby interior. Obviously, seats are the most important things to look at because PVC ones can only be replaced or repaired professionally, whereas leather seats are far more easily restored. Damage to the leather is the most serious problem, but this can be repaired, and the more common faults of split seams and scuffed areas can be greatly improved with a little hard work. Renovation kits are available which, properly used, can work wonders for tired leather, so don't be put off by dirty or scruffy leather trim, just make allowance for it when negotiating.

Headlining calls for special attention, but it can be replaced at quite a reasonable cost. However, look out for stains around the lower edge of the rear window, a sign of water leaks which may still exist. Like other Jaguar models, the compact saloons can suffer from rust beneath the headlining, caused by years of condensation; I have seen some very rusted examples, particularly cars with sunroofs.

Door panels were made from hardboard and covered with vinyl, and the hardboard quickly distorted and rotted when it became damp, something which may not be apparent with the door trims still in place. In the past, this caused quite a problem, the vinyl cover being partly bonded to the hardboard, which meant that it was not possible to cut out a new backing for the existing trim. However, nowadays complete replacement units are available, as are many other bits of vinyl trim for the Mk IIs, but sadly, the earlier cars are not as well catered for.

Carpets can be expensive to replace, so beware of 'cheapo' tufted replacements. Also, look for wet patches as the Mk IIs especially were prone to leaks, water often dripping past the door seals and settling on the floor. Another source of wet floors is water leaking past the sealing, or closing panels, at the rear of the front wings and trickling down the sides of the trim panels to settle on the front floorpan.

Refinishing the interior wood trim on a Jaguar is not a difficult or expensive job. I have achieved good results with French polish, a material I enjoy working with, but many other products are now on sale which are easy to use. It is best to remove everything but the dash, but on cars where the top rail is separate, remove it, and then either remove or mask the instruments and use a water washable stripper. Patience is more valuable than anything else, and I suggest you experiment with the finish on a small bit of scrap wood before you attack any of the important parts. Having this work done by a professional restorer can be very expensive, and of course you would have to remove all the parts, including the dash, as well as deliver, collect and refit them. So owners who feel uncertain about undertaking major mechanical or body work will probably find that they can achieve miracles with an untidy interior and get a lot of personal satisfaction doing so as well as save themselves a lot of money into the bargain.

Returning to the outside of the car and moving forward again, check the front suspension, remembering that testing properly for play in all the steering joints is really a job for someone really experienced, but driving the car is of course the only way to get a good overall impression of its handling. Expect the steering to be fairly heavy but not unduly stiff, and very precise and free from wander. At the same time, check the brakes; you will find that the pedal pressure will be higher than for a modern vehicle, but the car should pull up quickly and in a straight line.

A rusty front suspension will be an indication that the car has been standing for some time, in which case expect to have to renew balljoints, shock absorbers, etc, as Jaguars do not seem to benefit from being out of use for long periods. Check that the Metalastic mounting blocks have not disintegrated and be wary of assemblies which have been freshly painted; it is not unknown for rusty or otherwise worn front assemblies to be blast cleaned, then masked off and painted, giving the impression that the unit has been reconditioned.

Steering and idler boxes give little trouble and some boxes have a means for adjusting for wear. The column has two rubber universal joints, which should be examined for wear or disintegration, which can often be caused by oil eating into the rubber.

The XK engine is well-engineered and should run for a high mileage before needing a major overhaul. However, Jaguar engines were designed to have regular oil changes, and all too few of them received this treatment in later years. With the engine warm, and operating the throttle from under the bonnet, it is possible to reproduce most of the noises the engine will produce under load. For example, at lower revs you can hear a worn timing chain; top chains can be replaced at reasonable cost if too worn to be adjusted, but the replacement of a

Mk I   **1956**

bottom chain means that the engine will have to come out.

Camshafts should not be noisy, but a certain amount of rattle is quite normal. However, my own preference is for the cams to be so adjusted as to make them almost silent. To an experienced ear, big-end or main bearing noise on an XK unit is heard readily, and a certain amount of rumble can always be heard from them at close quarters, but if the oil pressure is adequate – about 40psi at high revs and about 20psi on tickover – there cannot be a lot wrong. However, it is worth remembering that whereas the oil gauges of earlier cars worked via a copper pipe, later cars had electrically driven gauges, which skilled hands can 'doctor' to give a higher reading. Expect to see oil leaks in moderation and traces of oil burning, especially on 3.8s, but an engine which breathes fumes has been worked hard and neglected.

Gearboxes fitted to older, pre-1965 cars will be quite noisy in first and reverse gears, which was the case when they were new and is part of their charm. But the noise should be no more than a low growl and the 'box should change gear smoothly, although it will not respond to fast changes and it will be easy to 'beat' the synchro. The later all-synchro boxes are easily identified by their thicker and longer gear-lever topped with a round black knob, and these should give smooth and quite positive changes and be quieter in operation. Clutches should be free of judder on takeoff, which is often a sign of a worn plate, and I would check for clutch slip by dipping the pedal with the car pulling hard in third gear; an unworn clutch will bite again at once without any trace of spin.

A final piece of advice: make your test drive as long as you are able and take in as many different traffic conditions as possible. The Mk Is and Mk IIs can be pleasant and exhilarating cars to drive, but unless you are used to driving cars of this type they can be hard work, and very tiring after a while. But should you buy one, and do so because you like the car rather than its investment value, I promise you that you will grow to love it and you will probably enjoy every moment you spend driving it, working on it, or even just talking about it. It is only fair to mention, though, that keeping one of these cars in good order takes both enthusiasm and at times a very deep pocket. In this connection, I would strongly advise joining one of the Jaguar clubs and meeting as many other owners as possible as such contacts can be invaluable for tracking down an elusive part or offering some urgently needed advice.

I certainly enjoyed my ownership of the compact Jaguars. What a wonderful experience they offered as they accelerated down a motorway, feeling the back end tuck down as the front end lifted under the surge of power, with the speedo needle rapidly swinging round the dial to, in those derestricted days, 100mph and beyond. True sports saloons, they were a new concept when they were designed and, to my mind, nothing has ever quite taken their place.

Mk II   **1960**

CHAPTER 5

XKs and E-types

"Today, there are examples on sale, fully restored and in almost as-new condition, at far less than the cost of their rebuild."

Although the majority of Jaguars I have owned or worked on have been saloons of one sort or another, quite a few sportscars have come my way, and looking back on them now I find that I still have quite mixed feelings about them. When they were good they were very good, but all too many of them were far from good, and some were downright awful, probably in many instances because they were difficult to work on and in consequence had been neglected by previous owners.

The first Jaguar sports I had any association with was an SS100. It was owned by a chap called Harry, who was then in his early forties and felt duty bound to keep it even though in reality he would have much preferred it to have been something like a Jaguar 1½-litre saloon. It appears that while he was away in the Navy on war service his father had been able to acquire the car, apparently still unregistered, and had stored it throughout the war before giving it to him in 1946 as a belated 21st birthday present.

Duly grateful, Harry used it regularly at first, but then, when he could afford a saloon for everyday use, he reserved the SS100 for occasional drives in the summer. So every spring I would see it emerge after its winter hibernation, and I think I can say that I never saw it without the hood off. It was finished in a dark metallic grey and I recall the seats were either black or a very dark blue. Also, I cannot remember whether it was a 2½ or a 3½-litre, but I fancy it was the former.

I drove the car on a number of occasions, and of course having covered such a low mileage it was in first class order, yet the two most lasting memories of this car were that it had a noisy engine and there was the ever-present smell of fumes, which seemed to enter the cockpit from under the gearbox cowling. When I moved house I lost touch with Harry, and later, when he and his family also left the district, the car went with them for he had vowed that he would never sell the SS100, or certainly not during his father's lifetime. My one regret is that I never took a photograph of this car – but then, who did in those days?

I must have been about six years old when I saw an XK120 for the first time on display in a London showroom, and I distinctly recall not being very impressed with its futuristic lines, which I thought smacked of a Dan Dare adventure. But of course tastes change quickly that early in life, and I grew up liking the XK very much indeed.

The problem was that I was still under 21 years of age when I bought my first one, and my insurance agent told me that I didn't have a cat in hell's chance of getting it covered! The car had been advertised in the local paper for several weeks: 'Jaguar sports, taxed and MoT, 1954 model, VGC, £120', but mine was the first serious inquiry about it. It was for sale because the owner, who had a Rover for daily use and drove a Jaguar for pleasure, was about to buy an E-type.

The XK was immaculate, having been well looked after by both its owners. It was an ivory-coloured drophead with plain tan interior and it had wire wheels with newish tyres, a

My insurance agent told me I didn't have a cat in hell's chance of getting it covered.

radio and many other well chosen accessories. I drove the car and loved it and was eagerly looking forward to taking it home. But the vendor, who must have been one of the most honest men I have ever met, realized that insurance would have been impossible, so he made me a most generous offer. Seeing my enthusiasm for the car, he said that for £85 I could take it, and he would name me as a driver on his policy for seven days. At the end of that time, if I had still been unable to insure the car, I should return it and he would refund the purchase price, unless of course it had been damaged while it was in my care. So I drove 'my' XK, hood up, hood down, for many enjoyable miles that weekend until my insurance agent, a very helpful man, nearly fell off his chair with laughter when I told him what I had done. The only deal he could get for a 19-year-old would have cost me about £150 for Road Traffic Act cover only – the minimum legal requirement – and even then there would have been a hefty excess, to be paid in advance. I even considered storing the car for a couple of years, but decided against this, so sadly I returned the XK to its former owner. A few months later the drophead found an enthusiastic new owner and it went back into regular use, but after a time I lost trace of it. I hope it has survived.

For a car that was intended to be a limited-production model with aluminium-panelled bodywork, the XK120 turned out to be a resounding success, with over 12,000 (nearly all of them steel-bodied) being built in the three body styles. Of course, there was not another production car in the world to match their performance, let alone their price, but it saddened me that so many of them fell into the wrong hands relatively early in their lives.

Most of the criticism of XKs comes from those who have had cause to own or drive cars which had been neglected and ill maintained, which was the fate of so many of them, often after only three or four years of use. These neglected XKs could be a deathtrap, whereas a well maintained one could be such a joy to drive.

One would have thought that cars like XKs would only have been bought by people who genuinely cared for them because, after all, they were not the most practical car for everyday use with their restricted room, far from brilliant weather protection or visibility, particularly with an aged hood and screens, and petrol consumption which could be quite horrific.

Yet I recall sad looking XKs being used as everyday hacks, one car in particular, which had such a bad case of door drop that both doors had been screwed to the body with metal brackets; the owner made a Le Mans-type entry by jumping over the side, and if the weather was bad he put the hood up from inside the car! The end for this car, which was brush painted in bright blue, came when the police pulled it up for a long overdue spot check, the mile-long list of faults which were revealed resulting in him being told to tow the car home. As he normally parked it in the street the XK was promptly dumped in a cinema carpark, but it was moved on and panic set in after the car was given its marching orders from the last available carpark. I delighted in telling this tiresome person that, far from buying his car, I would not accept it as a gift!

The XK120 was built around a substantial chassis and rust was not normally a problem for the first few years, but a nine-year-old car I owned required major work on the rear chassis-frame where mud had become trapped between the chassis and the petrol tank; this is probably the chassis' most vulnerable point, not least because it is well shielded from view. Other hidden rust areas are adjacent to the body mountings at the sides of the main frame and on the top of the chassis where mud and water have collected between the chassis and the body. The close proximity of body and chassis means that it is almost impossible to check an XK120's chassis properly for rust when the body is in place.

The XK120's rear wings are fixed by bolts, but all other sections of the main body are welded. The body itself comprises front-end and rear-end assemblies, the two parts being

The entire rear end of the roadster body had been removed and timbers had been fixed to the rear chassis to form a simple pickup truck base.

welded to the front and rear ends of the sill assembly. The result is a rigid bodyshell which was mounted in one piece and in theory should also be removable as a unit. This was probably quite feasible on nearly new cars, but with the possible exception of the fixed-head coupe, I suggest the best option is to first remove the sill assembly and then the front and rear sections separately, bearing in mind that the open cars were partly wood-framed.

Unfortunately, an XK120 can be expected to rot just about anywhere, and although some cars had an alloy bonnet, doors and bootlid, the rest of the metalwork was steel, and repairs to any part of the body can be quite complicated due to the method of construction. The front wings, for example, form part of the front-end assembly, which was built on a jig at the factory, so any new metal welded in must fit precisely. It is often an advantage to fit new panels or repair sections while the body – or what is left of it – is still fixed to the chassis, alignment being so critical. If I were removing body from chassis I would certainly carry out the necessary welded repairs before disturbing the body sections. But major body or chassis work on an XK120 is not the sort of task that even the most skilled amateur should tackle without first talking to someone who is familiar with the problems that can arise. The expense and complexity of this work is why so many XK restorations are abandoned, while the later XK140s and 150s can present even bigger headaches.

One of my XK120s came to me quite by accident. I discovered it by chance at a local farm, where it had been backed into a stall of a disused stable so that just its front end was visible. Partly sheeted up, the car had stood there collecting dust for a couple of years; the owner now wanted to sell it, but he suggested I uncover it properly before making up my mind. It was good advice! The entire rear end of the roadster body had been removed, and

The sump can be removed with the engine *in situ*, and as with the Mk VII, so can the pistons, conrods and timing chains.

behind the doors and seats, which were still in place, timbers had been fixed to the rear chassis to form a simple pickup truck base. The idea had been to construct a truck for carrying milk churns, but somehow the job was never finished.

The rear body section, which had seriously rotted, was now out on the scrap pile that most farmers seem to have, yet the front end of the vehicle was still very solid and free from rust. It seemed as though I had arrived just in time because the farmer was intending the very next day to push the XK out and cut it up for scrap metal. But instead he sold the remains to me for £10, which also covered the loan of a tractor to tow it to my workshop about a mile away.

Sometimes it is possible to look at an engine and know instinctively that it is a good one, and this was the case with this XK, which was free from oil leaks. After lubricating the bores and turning the engine by hand to free things up, it was no trouble to get it running, and sure enough it was a sweet sounding engine with good oil pressure. At the time, a good XK120 could be bought for less than £100, so restoring this one was out of the question. But I was determined to save it if I could, and in the end it went to someone in need of a front body section and a good engine.

Whilst body and chassis repairs can be time-consuming, heartbreaking and capable of swallowing up huge amounts of money, most mechanical parts for the XK120 are very similar to the Mk VII's and repairs and restoration quite straightforward. The sump can be removed with the engine *in situ*, and as with the Mk VII, so can the pistons, conrods and timing chains. The engine and gearbox can be removed as a unit, and although it is possible to remove just the gearbox from inside the car, I once took out an XK120's 'box this way and well remember the difficulty of working with such a heavy item in a very cramped space. In my view, the quickest way to gain access to the gearbox or clutch is after removing them with the engine through the front; anyone who has tried to refit a gearbox via the inside of an XK120 is sure to agree with me!

One day I came across a roadster at a garage I frequented which looked to be a sound car. It had been painted very well in a non-original metallic blue and it had a tidy red interior, a reasonable hood and a set of tyres that were just about legal. It had been taken in part exchange and was suffering from clutch slip, but it was offered to me for £35, the doors didn't drop, it had an MoT certificate and it could be driven home under its own power, so I decided to buy it.

The car had very little wrong with it, and after doing the clutch, putting on some good tyres, servicing it and checking everything over properly I used it myself for a while. It performed very well and gave me no problems, but XK120 roadsters are not suited to daily use and town centre parking, so I decided to part with it after a few months. It seems strange now, but when I put the car up for sale no-one turned up to look at it; XKs, even nice ones, were just about unsaleable at any price! In the end I did find an enthusiastic buyer, and I think he paid me about £65 for it, which was not a lot for a car that needed nothing spending on it.

The XK's front suspension is basically the same as that of the Mk VII except for the anti-roll bar, which on the XK is fixed forward of the lower wishbone. The steering is also very like that of the Mk VII, other than the mounting of the steering box. Removal of this entails partly stripping the dash, dismantling various under-bonnet components, then extracting the unit complete with the column from underneath the front wing.

The rear suspension employs semi-elliptic springs with hydraulic lever-type shock absorbers, the axle fitting on top of the springs and under the chassis, with the fuel tank close by, mounted within the chassis. Axle removal is supposed to be quite easy, but I have only had to do this once on an XK, a friend's car, in order to replace one with excessive backlash, caused almost certainly by towing a heavy boat. As with the Mk VII, I found it much easier to do this job by lowering the springs. In fact in this case I removed the axle and springs together.

Although the XK120s were criticised right from the beginning for poor brakes, and in particular for brake fade, I must say that I always considered them adequate for the car. However, I have never relied on brakes alone to slow a car, and I much enjoy using the gears on one like the XK to help with the slowing down process. I have to admit, though, that the early XKs in particular were prone to brake fade if you used them really hard.

The brakes were mounted in 12in drums, hydraulically operated, of course, the master-cylinder being mounted on the chassis and operated by a pushrod from the pedal. At first all four drums had provision for adjustment, but later front brakes were self-adjusting and subsequently a tandem master-cylinder was provided. Surprisingly, servo-assistance was never a standard feature. I found the brakes easy to maintain, and the master-cylinder could be dismantled for overhaul, while the handbrake was well-designed and usually efficient.

By the time they were 10 years old, I must have been one of the very few people around who still really liked and appreciated the XK120, despite their by now dated looks. At that time, most who bought them did so because they were just another cheap big sportscar, and they were all too quick to dump them when any real expense loomed. On the other hand, there were still a few who had bought their cars new and were prepared to continue using them as weekend runabouts, rather than offer them in part-exchange, because they were well aware of their low value. My only XK150 (I never actually owned an XK140) came from such a person.

The main reason why the XK140 escaped me was simply that the opportunity to buy one never presented itself at the right time, although I must say that I always thought this model never looked right with its clumsy bumpers. Technically, of course, the car was an improvement on the 120 with its rack-and-pinion steering and the option of overdrive, but it retained drum brakes and was based on a very similar chassis, although the engine was mounted further forward to improve cockpit room. Also, being so similar, it suffered the same maladies as the earlier car, including its tendencies to corrosion, though neither model could match the 150's ability when it came to gathering rot!

From the day I first saw one, I loved the XK150, because to my eye with this car the earlier styling had been greatly improved, giving the new model graceful lines and an elegant appearance. I know that not everyone agrees with me, but styling has always been a subjective matter. Of course, the 150 was also a more practical car with its wider body and roomier interior, and the replacement of the walnut trim with leather was another improvement, but best of all, the car had disc brakes all round.

In spite of the model's reputation for rusting, I was most fortunate that my XK150, a 1959 3.4, was completely corrosion-free when I bought it, even though it was then 12 years old, and the only mechanical work it required was a gearbox swap. Ironically, it was probably because of its serious gearbox fault that the car was otherwise in such good condition. The owner had not considered it worth paying for such an expensive repair and so had stored the car for a considerable time in a dry greenhouse, and he approached me because he had finally decided to find a good home for it. I must say I went along to see it in a most disinterested mood because the last thing I wanted at that time was yet another old Jaguar.

It was a fixed-head coupe in dark grey with a navy blue interior, and the first thing that struck me about it was how well the car stood on its well-shod painted wire wheels, despite being idle for so long. It had obviously been well looked after and I was delighted to find that all the metalwork was as solid as a rock, and there was not even any mud in evidence to hide anything. When I lifted the bonnet there was another surprise because there sat triple SU carburettors. The seller told me that he had bought the car from its original owner, and to the best of his knowledge it had left the factory with the three carbs installed. When the engine was fired up it sounded both sweet and powerful, and I made up my mind right away that a car as good as this one should be back on the road.

I didn't relish the prospect of a gearbox change, but at least I had done worse jobs. The

It must have been an epidemic . . . . !

engine and gearbox came out as one, although it was a tight squeeze, and the damaged 'box was discarded. In its place I fitted a later all-synchro unit, which I seem to recall came from an S-type. I also remember having to get the gear-lever altered into the cranked shape unique to XKs and then having it replated. Ahead of the 'box, of course, went a new clutch, even though this was still a low-mileage car. Because the car had stood for so long, the brakes were binding, but I soon freed them off, and after a thorough checkover and service the MoT test was no problem, after which I steam-cleaned and oil-sprayed the entire underside.

The modern 'box made this car an absolute pleasure to drive, and I cared little about the criticism for not keeping it to its original specification. If a modification can make a car easier, safer or more pleasant to use I cannot see why there can be any valid objection. I ran the XK150 for about two years, although it was not used every day, and in the end I sold it quite cheaply, just about a year before XK prices went through the roof! It is my firm intention one day to own another one, but I shall take a great deal of care before writing out a cheque.

Despite my good fortune with the dark grey car, I am all too well aware of the XK150's structural weaknesses and of the skill of those who seek to camouflage them, so I shall almost certainly be accompanied by someone who is an acknowledged expert on this particular model, and I will be especially wary of any car that has been returned from the US, particularly if it has been either partly or fully restored.

Some time ago I met a self-styled enthusiast who makes a nice living shipping over XKs in any state and then carefully preparing them for sale as part-completed restoration projects. He is an expert at 'stitching' body panels together in such a way as to make it look as though the car needs very little finishing off. Body sections are cannibalized from one body and grafted onto another so that two or even three rotten shells can go into making a complete and fairly rust-free one. Take my word for it, there are a lot of XKs about that have been built up this way with the aid of plenty of quick welds and body filler, followed by a nice coat of paint.

A really nice, genuine XK can be a wonderful car, well able to hold its own even on the busy roads of the Nineties, and above all these are driver's cars, cars to be used, not for investors to store away. But a bad one can be a never-ending nightmare. The late Sixties and early Seventies were a particularly bad time for them, for during that period they came off the road in large numbers, usually because restoration work proved to be beyond the skill of their owners and was too expensive to put in the hands of a professional.

I think my saddest memory of an XK is of a blue 120 fixed-head coupe which I viewed from a window of a slow-moving train somewhere in the Midlands. Its tyres were flat, its windows broken, the bonnet and boot were both up and the roof was dented. It had been

XK140   **1956**

abandoned on waste land and had become the plaything of mischievous children. No doubt today it would have been a magnet for another group altogether, the hunters of valued spares.

It is strange how attitudes change with time. In 1961, the E-type was hailed as one of the most desirable and attractive cars in the world, and this image persisted through to the late Sixties. But soon afterwards, E-types were suddenly out of fashion and became neglected and in many instances unwanted. During the Seventies they were in demand mainly by impoverished would-be playboys, hoping that their smoky and well used car would be mistaken for a later and more valuable model. Most pub, night club and golf carparks would usually sport an E-type or two.

But in the late Seventies and early Eighties, the trendies decided that they were 'the' classic car to own, preferably in red with black trim, and in consequence prices went through the roof. Then, after some of these speculators had lost interest, and in many cases quite a lot of money, prices tumbled again to more realistic levels, which meant that the true enthusiast once again could afford to buy one. Today, there are examples on sale, fully restored and in almost as-new condition, at far less than the cost of their rebuild.

However, I have to admit that I have never been a great enthusiast of these cars. For me, the style quickly dated and an E-type today certainly looks old-fashioned from certain angles. The cars had two main problems: they were often badly neglected, and they rotted in the most alarming manner. In recent years, a full range of body panels, even full shells, have become available, facilitating the restoration of even the worst 'basket cases', but at a high cost. In earlier times, when only sills and a few part repair panels were made, many of the cars were bodged in the most dangerous manner because, even when prices were at their lowest ebb, it was always possible to sell an E-type which had an MoT certificate and a bright but 'cheapo' respray.

The first one I owned was more or less thrust upon me. It stood, with its rear end high on axle stands, at the back of a vast workshop of a garage I used to visit. It was a very early roadster in a sort of metallic British Racing Green, and I made the mistake of expressing an interest in it, because within a week it was standing in my own workshop!

It was this garage owner's personal project, but he had never got around to finishing it. The rear suspension unit had been removed in order to weld the corroded mounting points, and I was at a loss to see how the car could be moved with the job unfinished, but delivery was included in the price, and as promised it was duly transported to my premises. I arrived there to find it already up on a pair of stands, completely undamaged, with the subframe on the floor beside it, and to this day I cannot imagine how the 'miracle' was performed.

The car had cost me £90, and welding the new metal that was required around the

XK150   **1958**

mounting points took many hours, while refitting the independent rear suspension after a minor brake overhaul also proved to be tiresome work, but it was worth the effort to do the job properly. Apart from attending to the front brakes and carrying out a full service, the only other work required was some minor welding on one sill, the rest of the car being in excellent order.

There is no disputing that a good 3.8-litre E-type, like that one, is a very fast car, and although I never put it to the test, had I done so I imagine it would have got fairly close to the 150mph top speed that some people claimed for it. I had only two complaints about that car, one being the usual one about the gearbox, and the other the cramped, almost claustrophobic, interior when the hood was erected. These things apart, and notwithstanding my reticence about E-types in general, I enjoyed that car very much, especially on a warm day with the hood down, and I used it purely for pleasure during that summer.

When I decided it was time to part with it I advertised it for £350, which would have been just about what it had cost me in total, but having declined to sell the car to two unsuitable buyers, one of whom became quite nasty, I found it a good home and let it go for, I think, £325. It seems incredible in the Nineties that in those days a 3.8 E-type roadster, less than 10 years old and in first-class order, in need of no attention whatsoever, could be put on sale for such a low sum and attract only three potential buyers.

The E-type must be the most difficult Jaguar of all to work on. Even jacking one up is not easy, and despite the good facilities at my disposal I found what should have been quite minor tasks to be very awkward. Although the roadster I have already mentioned required relatively little work, I did get to learn a lot about E-type construction when I dismantled a very dangerous example for disposal.

Corrosion was the big problem on these cars right from the beginning. Most of them seemed to rot everywhere, yet strangely, some examples, like my roadster, resisted rust quite well. Body construction of both the coupe and the roadster involved a large number of small panels, and many of these are welded, but this does make part repairs possible where the corrosion is limited.

The front frame assembly, which is made from square-section tube and is fixed to the main body structure, supports the engine, the front suspension and the massive lift-up bonnet. The frame sections are bolted together so that should any of them become accident-damaged they can be easily replaced. The parts of this frame, therefore, should never be welded, while alignment of the frame to the main body is absolutely critical.

The front suspension, which works in conjunction with rack-and-pinion steering, consists of wishbones and torsion bars with telescopic dampers and does an excellent job if properly maintained, but repairs can be very expensive. As I have already indicated, the rear subframe, which provides the mounting for the rear suspension as well as the final drive and brakes, is removable as a complete assembly in the event of major repair work being necessary.

One problem associated with the otherwise powerful inboard-mounted disc brakes is that, being exposed to the weather, their performance can deteriorate in severe conditions. Early cars were equipped with an adjustable handbrake, the calipers being accessible via a panel in the boot floor, and although later cars were provided with a self-adjusting handbrake these were less than successful.

A complicated item on the underside of these cars is the exhaust system, which involves twin pipes and silencers running from front to rear. There seems to be widely divergent opinions as regards exhaust life, some owners I have talked to claiming that the exhausts last for years, whereas others have told me they expect to change them almost annually, but of one thing they are all agreed: replacement systems are very expensive! The first cars used the 265bhp 'gold top' engine straight out of the XK150S, coupled to the old gearbox with its slow change, but the later 4.2-litre cars had a much nicer 'box, although it seemed to lack the strength of the earlier unit. Incidentally, one of the items I particularly liked about the E-

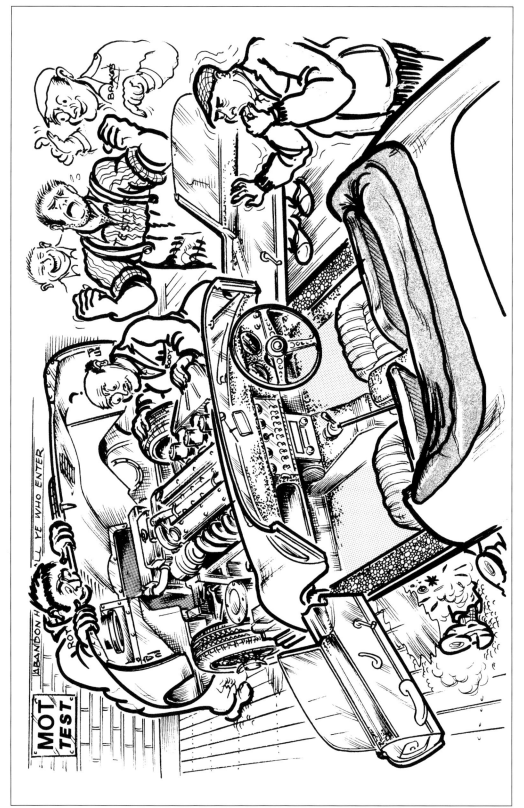

The E-type must be the most difficult Jaguar of all to work on.

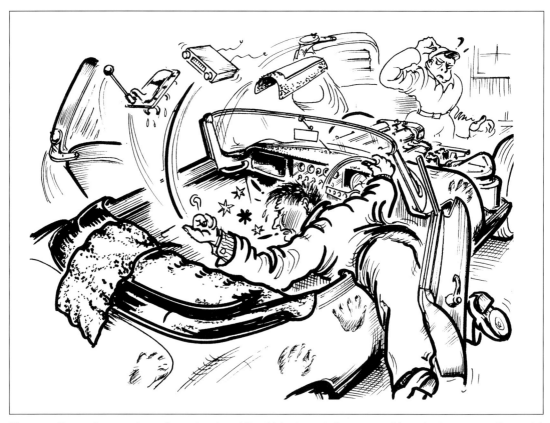

Then . . . the seats, carpets, radio and various bits of trim have to be removed in order to unscrew the metal propshaft and gearbox covers.

type was its manual choke control, which I thought was very practical.

Should you be contemplating removal of the engine, be prepared for some hard work! After taking off the full-width bonnet section and the radiator, you must next remove the crankshaft pulley, the oil filter and various other items. Then, having removed the grime from your hands and donned clean overalls, you have to begin work inside the car because the seats, carpets, radio and various bits of trim have to be removed in order to unscrew the metal propshaft and gearbox covers. Only then can you remove the gearbox extension, the rear mounting, the propshaft, etc. Finally, when everything has been undone, there remains the problem of easing the heavy unit out past the tubular frame. This procedure is also required should it be necessary to remove the gearbox or gain access to the clutch.

Almost everything about these cars is complicated and expensive to restore, and even the interior, which looks relatively spartan in comparison with other Jaguar models, can be very costly to refurbish. As a result of this, many cars will have had crude repairs carried out in the past, and the story of one car I owned illustrates how clever some people can be in making a bad example look quite attractive on the surface.

It began with an Austin-Healey 100/4, which I rescued from an uncaring owner and after refurbishing it used for everyday transport. But it was impractical, so I sold it and took a Mini-Cooper in part-exchange, which I then used for a while before advertising it for sale again. A Mini enthusiast, keen to buy a good Cooper, responded, a price was agreed, and I offered to deliver it to his home, some 30 miles away. He was delighted by this because by now he knew of my interest in Jaguars and hoped that I might be able to extend this to one which had become a great embarrassment to him.

In his garage stood a 1963 fixed-head E-type in red which, viewed from a few feet away, looked quite nice. But a closer look told a different story. It was an obvious respray, in one of those nasty paints which give an instant and too bright a gloss, and it hid a lot of trouble. He had bought the Jaguar from a car lot over a year earlier and it had been nothing but trouble ever since – oil leaks, water leaks, brake problems, just about everything. Then, when its MoT was due, the local garage had refused to take it for a road test because the car was deemed to be too dangerous; there was serious body rot and the brake pipes were badly corroded. So he was now offering me the chance to buy it for spares for £50.

Because the car had a good bonnet section I did so, thinking that if ever I bought another E-type, here would be a good source of spares. The car came home on a trailer, and a quick drive along some lanes told me that the rather smoky engine was still quite lively, the gearbox was good and so was the diff. But a quick look at the underside was sufficient to convince me that it should be broken up and never allowed to go back on the road, even though I was to receive several offers for it while it lay in the corner of the workshop awaiting its fate.

Removal of the bonnet revealed this to be a newish and genuine Jaguar-supplied one, but it soon became obvious that the car had been in a heavy collision as the front frame had been repaired by welding in sections of mismatched tubing. The next job was the removal of the engine and gearbox, followed by the rear suspension assembly and the exhaust system. Later on, the gutted shell was turned onto its roof to reveal the full horrors.

Most of the sills, which are very important on these cars, had rotted severely and cover sills had been tacked on over the remains of the originals, and inside, where rust had eaten away between the inner sills and the floorpan, the gaps had been filled with matting and resin. No wonder the door gaps had been so uneven, and it was a miracle that the car hadn't simply folded up during use.

Other parts of the underside had been botched with bits of tinplate pop-riveted over holes, followed by a heavy coat of underseal. A rusted mounting point for the rear suspension had been bodged with angle-iron and a rubber mounting had disintegrated so that only a tyre lever was needed to separate the assembly from the body. The brakes could not have worked properly for ages, so badly seized were some of the components. The car had been a deathtrap because it would still have been capable of 120mph with not a chance of it being stoppable in an emergency. Whoever had given that car its last MoT certificate should have been strung up, along with the person who had sold it to its last owner and whoever had been responsible for bodging the repairs. The engine found a home in another E-type eventually, and the other usable parts were gradually disposed of.

I never did have another E-type, but I did have some fun bidding for one a while later. Auctions are not places I like, having always regarded them as a means of getting people to pay silly prices for otherwise unsaleable cars. It hasn't escaped me that cars put through 'classic' auctions not only achieve higher prices than they probably deserve, but the organizers have also contrived to persuade both the buyer and the seller to pay them a commission on top, so it strikes me that there is only one real winner, and it's not the customer. However, the last time I attended one was to look at an early E-type fixed-head which, although right-hand drive, had recently returned from overseas and accordingly had a current registration number. It seemed like a very clean car, but a quick look under the bonnet was sufficient for me and I retired to the back of the hall to watch the bidding, doing my best to keep a straight face.

I was not intending to bid at all, but present at the sale and showing some interest in the car were a pair of rather overbearing know-it-all enthusiasts and an example of that even lower form of animal life, the part-time dealer who disguises himself as a genuine car-lover. So I let them start the bidding, then slipped in a couple of bids myself to jolly things along before withdrawing to let them get on with it.

Eventually, one of them ended up paying over £800 for something that he could have

It was a miracle the car hadn't folded up . . .

bought from an advertisement in *Motor Sport* for at least £300 less. The purchaser was delighted, boasting to me that you have to pay a proper price for the car you want, so I handed him my card, saying that if ever he needed an E-type engine he might care to ring me. Neither he, nor presumably the other two bidders, had noticed that nestling in the front of the car he had just bought was a 2.4-litre engine, complete with Solex carburettors!

From all the E-types I have owned or driven, ideally I would choose a 3.8 fitted with a later gearbox, while the early 4.2s were also nice cars, but I think the later Series 1⅛s or Series 2s were less attractive. But my advice to anyone contemplating the purchase of any of them is not to even consider it until you have someone lined up who can give you a reliable second opinion based on genuine expertise. This advice is valid for any Jaguar model, but never more so than for the E-type.

E-type   **1971**

CHAPTER 6

XJ6s and XJSs

"I found there was very little to fault about the driving performance of the Series 3, but my, can they rot."

I have long considered the Jaguar XJ6 to be a masterpiece of both design and engineering. When it appeared in 1968 it also offered wonderful value for money, and it certainly achieved something remarkable in appealing to such a wide range of Jaguar buyers, which enabled the company to reduce its range substantially without losing sales. During five years of production around 79,000 Series 1s were produced, the majority of them with the 4.2-litre engine, sales of the rather underpowered 2.8 being somewhat limited.

The Series 2 was essentially a facelift model, the most visible differences being the replacement of the Series 1's large and rather ugly grille with a much neater one, and a raised front bumper, which now had the side/indicator lights mounted below it. The result was a much nicer looking car. These and other modifications, including an updated interior, helped to make the Series 2 a big success.

The 4.2-litre engine was retained, but the sickly 2.8 was replaced by a 3.4-litre unit. However, buyers who thought that the 3.4 badge stood for high performance were to be disappointed, for this particular 3.4 was an economy low-compression version, running with Stromberg carburettors. By now, Jaguar was part of the British Leyland conglomerate, and the BL influence was beginning to show. Many 'universal' components would be seen on Jaguars from now on, and another indication of declining quality and exclusivity was the increasing use of standard BL colours, many of which were totally unsuited to Jaguars.

Later, the two-door coupe version was introduced, but there were a number of teething troubles, production was delayed, and the model never proved popular, accounting for only about 7,000 of the 78,000 six-cylinder Jaguars produced during that period.

I liked the Series 2 very much, and I kept mine for a long time after the model had been replaced by the Series 3. It took me quite a time to accept the modified lines of the new model, the roofline in particular seeming to me to be very un-Jaguar in style. But at least the Series 3 4.2s came with fuel injection, but as for the 3.4s, the less said the better. These days, of course, the Series 3s are attracting greater interest as the last of the XK-engined Jaguars, and I have noticed some very over-priced examples in the marketplace, although whether or not they find buyers at those prices is another matter.

The majority of XJ6s were supplied with automatic transmission, which means that the desirable and pleasant manual 'boxes – both the early version with four speeds and overdrive, or the later five-speeder – are quite rare.

The V12 version was first offered in 1973, and despite its excessive thirst it sold quite well. Although I have driven these cars I have never actually owned one, so I cannot comment from that standpoint, but many owners have told me that an underworked V12 tends to produce a black sludge, the 'black death', the build-up of which is impossible to remove without stripping the engine. Therefore, any engine with this afflication is probably best left alone, and I am told that the problem is not one that only applies to

Sills are amongst the most common replacements, and they start to rot from the inside . . .

high-mileage cars.

As anyone who has experienced one will confirm, a really nice XJ6 is a delight to drive. I cannot think of any other car that can match the comfort and ride quality, or the superb roadholding, especially when you consider the Jaguar's size and weight, and with the 4.2-litre engine the performance is more than adequate.

But sadly, these cars rotted badly, and quite rapidly, no single part of the body assembly seeming able to escape the rust. I have seen XJs rot in the most strange places, such as around the petrol filler caps and even in the centre of the roof panel, indicating that poor quality metal was more likely the cause than the penetration of water. A rotted example can be costly and complicated to repair, even for someone with welding equipment, because XJs have lots of hidden places where rust can lurk unseen, as anyone who has replaced a sill will surely agree.

So maintenance and repair of an XJ is not easy, even with good facilities, and as is the case with most Jaguars, the sheer weight and bulk are a major problem, while the complexity of the brakes, suspension and steering only add to the difficulties.

Apart from the front wings, which are bolted on, the main body structure is welded. Most of the panels are quite large, and a considerable amount of overlap occurs, making the replacement of one panel quite difficult. Many part repair panels are available, and if these are of good quality, sound repairs can be achieved by a competent welder, but there are also some 'cheapo' panels of poor quality on the market, and in most cases getting these to fit is extremely difficult, if not impossible.

Sills are amongst the most common replacements, and they often start to rot from the inside, so things are usually serious by the time the rust shows through. The inner sills, which are structural, also form part of the floor and the seatbelt mounting. They really form the edges of the floorpan and extend under the car, so replacement is diffficult and complicated and is certainly not a job for the inexperienced or ill-equipped, for this panel also affects the alignment of the shell.

Floorpans can also rust away unseen, the worst places being along the edge of the inner seal and the front footwell; I have seen quite young cars with this problem. In fact, rather than list every rust area on an XJ6, it is probably easier to say that there is scarcely any part of it which is immune from the rust bug. For example, one car I saw not long ago, which had been rust-treated from new, still had the usual gaping hole where the rear valance meets the boot floor. So expect any nice-looking XJ to have plenty of filler; rust-free examples are extremely rare, and unless you know that the car in question has been repaired properly by an enthusiast, remember that – until recently, at least – expensive body restoration was simply not justified on cost grounds.

My first XJ was a late 2.8 with manual gearbox. It was finished in red with the light tan leather trim and matching vinyl roof. At the time the car was about four years old and it had been repossessed from its last owner. Despite not having been properly serviced for a long time, it was still in very good order, so I serviced and checked it over myself, then had it properly valeted.

The 2.8 had a reputation for burning valves and pistons, as well as being generally unreliable, but it transpired that my car had had some engine mods quite early in its life and as a result it performed reasonably well, and during my ownership of it it never gave me any trouble and was a delight to drive. Like the earlier Mk II 2.4s, here was a Jaguar with a relatively small engine and a heavy body, and so it was no more economical to run than the larger version. Apart from routine servicing, brake pads and a couple of tyres, this car needed nothing doing to it, it was remarkably rust-free, and I kept it that way with regular steam-cleaning and oil spray.

After about a year's use I traded the 2.8 for a 4.2 of about the same age, but sadly this bigger car was an automatic, which I dislike intensely, but at least the car had been well cared for. It was a pleasant shade of light blue, with dark leather trim, and in comparison with my previous car it went like the proverbial bat out of hell. But when the opportunity came to exchange it for a manual version – an L-registered 4.2 in white with red leather – I took it; suffice to say that the other party got the better of the deal.

This was when I got to know XJs quite well. The first problem was leaking tanks. Removing, cleaning and repairing them with resin meant that the car was off the road for quite a while, but I could guarantee that afterwards those tanks would outlast the car. Incidentally, this was one of several successful repairs I have made to corroded petrol tanks, using glassfibre matting and resin. The materials I used were supplied by a company engaged in making and repairing fuel tanks for boats, aircraft and racing machinery, so having been developed for these purposes they were safe to use. (Never use ordinary general-repair glassfibre for repairing fuel tanks as resins of this type are soluble in petrol.)

My next fright with this car was whilst driving along the M6 motorway at high speed in the outside lane. Suddenly the engine cut completely for a split second before picking up again, and although there was no lost momentum the episode certainly made my heart beat faster for a while. The next day, after a lengthy session on a Sun tuner failed to reveal any faults, I began to suspect the fuel system, believing that perhaps I had disturbed some sediment whilst removing the tanks. So I drained them, flushed them out, cleaned the lines, renewed the filters, cleaned the carburettors and discovered..... nothing!

After the car repeated its earlier antics I checked everything over time and time again, but by then I had lost confidence in it. It was only a chance meeting with another owner that led me to suspect the distributor. A strip down revealed that due to slight rust in the mechanism the advance and retard assembly might have momentarily seized. So an exchange unit was fitted, the timing properly set up and the problem never recurred, which meant that I felt fairly happy with the car again.

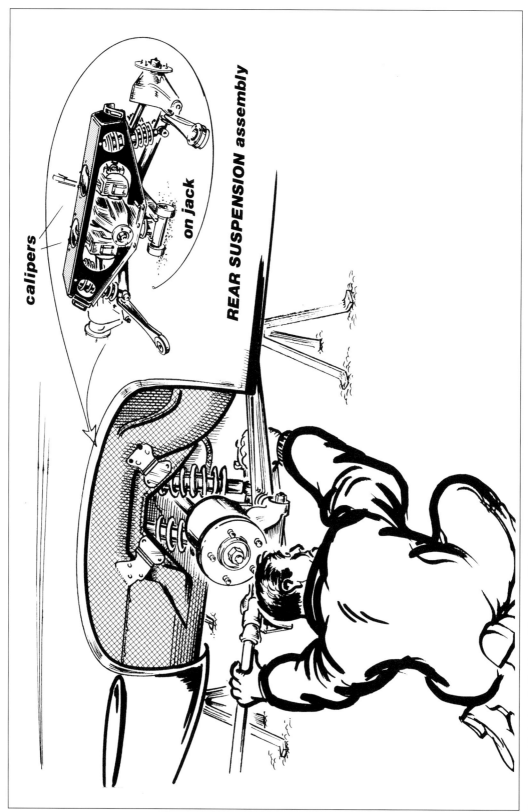

calipers

on jack

REAR SUSPENSION assembly

It was probably fortunate that I read the manual before trying to remove the rear calipers . . . .

XJ6   **1969**

But from the day I had brought it home, I had been less than happy with the car's brakes. Inspection of the front calipers confirmed that the pistons were sticking, which was not surprising bearing in mind that the car had been standing for some time. Removal of the calipers was not difficult and they were soon fitted with new seals and replaced. I always used the excellent Castrol/Girling brake rubber grease when assembling brake components, but like a lot of other useful products, after a time it seemed to disappear from the shelves.

It was probably fortunate that I read the manual before trying to remove the rear calipers, for the only proper way to do this on Series 1 XJ6s is to first lower the complete rear suspension assembly. This came as quite a surprise because it is a lengthy operation, during which the car must be supported on stands beneath the floorpan, and whilst this might be all right with a new and therefore solid car, I would be most reluctant to work beneath an older and rusted vehicle supported in this manner!

After an overhaul of both the disc and handbrake calipers, braking was just as a Jaguar's should be, and although the total cost of the pads and the overhaul kits was quite high, I estimate that I had done the complete job in about eight to 10 hours. Bearing in mind the inevitable problems caused by seized components on a car that was then about three years old, I doubt whether even an experienced garage could have done the work in much less time. I was just glad not to have been paying a full day's labour charge, plus the parts at full retail price. Also, I had enjoyed the involvement and the satisfaction of knowing that the job had been completed to my own standards.

Now the white 4.2 was in perfect order, and although I had probably spent around £300 on parts alone to bring the car up to standard, I was more than glad to have had the facilities and ability to carry out this work myself. Normally, parts and labour would have cost someone at least £1,000, which was not an inconsiderable sum in 1976/77, so no wonder so many Jaguars were very much neglected at the time. Of course, the expense involved was due at least in part to me being so fussy; liberal use of penetrating oil and a hammer would no doubt have freed off the brakes in order to squeeze the car through another MoT test, which is what many other owners would have done.

When I bought my first Series 2 XJ, I advertised this car in a local evening paper, and this resulted in the most unusual deal I have ever been involved in. The caller rang to ask for details, and after listening to an honest description and my reasons for selling the car, he asked if I would be willing to meet him the next day at a particular multi-storey car park. The moment I parked the car on the agreed high level, a middle-aged gent came to greet me, he looked around the car, then the interior, and asked to look under the bonnet and in the boot. He then suggested we sit in the car to count the money, which he carried in a black executive-type case. I asked if he would like to have a run round the town, but he declined the offer politely, explaining that he had watched the car as it had climbed the ramps, and that was good enough. My description had been most honest and he was happy to pay the asking price. So cash and documents were exchanged, and the new owner drove away. I still have the smart black case which he insisted I keep.

When a friend asked if he could bring his newly bought 2.8 along to my workshop and

I advertised this car in a local evening paper, and this resulted in the most unusual deal I have ever been involved in.

seek some advice he sounded worried, and not without good reason. He had bought the car at an auction. It was a Daimler version and it looked quite smart, but when he pulled into a service station for some fuel on the way home the garage owner recognized the number-plate as the one that had been on a car he had had in for an MoT test a few days earlier. He was also convinced that the car he had tested was not the one he was looking at now.

The Daimler had been resprayed in the original Sable colour, and it looked very presentable. However, two things struck me at once: the car leaked water very badly and it had been clocked. It just smelled water, which had been getting in where the floor had rusted away along the entire length of both sills. Tinplate had been pop-riveted over the gaps and then covered with underseal and then the carpet stuck back on top. The only solution would have been extensive welding, but this was something I did not wish to become involved with.

Obviously, the speedo was from another car because it was only showing about 40,000 miles and had been badly fitted. There were all the signs to indicate that this particular Daimler had done many more miles than this. I suggested that the only way out of my friend's dilemma was to put the car into another auction – preferably one further from home. This he did, and the car was duly sold, but at a loss. Then, within a week or two it showed up again, this time on a dealer's forecourt, wearing a very high price. What had happened about the corroded floor I knew not, and perhaps it was as well.

I only had one serious criticism of the early XJs, which was the lightness of the steering; at times it was so light that it almost felt as though the front wheels had left the ground. But this apart, I thought they were wonderful cars, at least in 4.2-litre form. But probably more than any other Jaguar, they instantly looked dated when the replacement model was announced. As a result, with the arrival of the Series 2, prices of the now obsolete Series 1 nose-dived.

My first Series 2 came my way very cheaply. It was also the last Jaguar on which I did any really extensive work. For some time, I had been finding this sort of work no longer a labour of love, and once this particular project was finished, I locked the workshop door and didn't go near the place again for nearly a year. After all the years spent bringing tired Jaguars and other cars back into an extended useful life I think I had had enough. These days I tend to have my cars serviced by others, even though this means that sometimes I cringe when I see badly fitted components, or oily marks on the paintwork, or have to listen to excuses as to why faults have remained undiagnosed.

My Series 2 had been parked on the driveway of a house which I drove past regularly, and obviously it had not been used for some time because the owner seemed to be running a later model. One day my curiosity got the better of me and I stopped to ask about the car. It was a 1976 model, which meant that it was not yet three years old, but it was finished in that awful shade of light maroon. However, it had an unmarked biscuit interior and factory-fitted chrome wheels.

The owner had bought it new, its mileage was still nominal and it had been serviced regularly. But it had been off the road for some time because there was a problem with the automatic gearbox. Faced with an extensive bill for a car which was due to be replaced soon anyway, he had decided to lease another car. He had always run Jaguars, beginning with a new 1½-litre, so we had a lot to chat about. Although he made it clear that the car would not drive, the engine started quickly and seemed to be running well, and he was offering it to me for a cash price that I found hard to believe. A day or so later the grimey 4.2 was being loaded onto a transporter.

My first task was to remove the engine and transmission. I had hoped to convert it to a manual gearbox, but the parts were so hard to find – and so expensive – that I decided to

My first task was to remove the engine and transmission . . .

refit a rebuilt automatic gearbox instead. Engine removal on an XJ is quite easy because with the massive bonnet out of the way there is plenty of room to move around, the only major difficulty being the great weight of the unit. The gearbox and torque converter were sent to a friendly specialist for appraisal, and in the meantime I decided to check the engine over and fit new timing chains. As this operation involved removing the head and sump I took the opportunity to examine the big-end and main bearings, and as both sets were unmarked they were re-used, but with new bolts and locknuts.

As the head seemed very clean, I did not disturb the valves, but merely cleaned the heads and ports. The cams were not worn, which meant that I had no need to remove them, thereby saving the trouble of resetting the valve clearances, etc. Although the chains were showing only slight wear I felt it was sensible to replace them, along with the tensioner. I also serviced the carbs and fitted a new AED unit.

The original gearbox was repaired at very little cost, and the converter was in good order, so I was saved any great expense. With the unit back in place the engine started easily, and once the carbs had been set up it sounded very sweet – ample reward for all my hard work and bruised hands. Once I had checked everything over, the car was taken for its first MoT test, which it passed, and then I took it for a long drive. It performed marvellously, driving just like a new car, and I returned home feeling very pleased that I had bought it.

The only thing I was unhappy about was the colour, and I decided there and then to do something about it. This 4.2 was going to be black. I knew that a colour change on an XJ would be a complicated job, but this car was worth the effort and I allowed myself a week to complete the work.

To do the colour change properly meant quite a lot of stripping. I removed the bootlid and bonnet, but left the doors in place after removing all the trim and then masked up the apertures. Following careful preparation, I painted the door edges, pillars, the inside of the engine bay and boot, and the undersides of the bonnet and bootlid. After 24 hours the bonnet and bootlid were refitted and the final preparation took place before applying the top coat. I chose a two-pack acrylic, my method in using this being to apply it wet on wet which, if done skilfully, achieves a good thickness of paint with no runs. This particular job turned out to be excellence itself; although quite often this type of paint looks too shiny at first, after a day or two it settles down.

Properly applied, these paints need no cutting back or polishing and look really superb, and this Jaguar looked as if black had been its factory colour. There is a great deal of satisfaction to be gained from a well done paint job, which more than makes up for the many hours of tedious and messy rubbing down. With the paintwork finished and the interior properly cleaned, the 4.2 looked and drove like a three-month-old car. It became my regular daily transport for a considerable time, and I enjoyed every moment I spent driving it.

This was the only Series 2 I ever owned for any length of time, and although I always intended to replace it some time with a manual gearbox version, a nice enough example never came my way. I did own a 3.4 briefly, which came as part of a debt, and I took ages to find a buyer for it. I also declined an offer to exchange my 4.2 for a coupe version, which was a slightly older car and although an excellent runner was a little tatty around the edges. These two-door cars never became the valuable commodity that many had predicted, and somehow to me they never looked quite right.

When the time came for me to buy a Series 3 – a 4.2 with a manual gearbox – the days had long gone of struggling with engines, seized brakes and other such niceties. It was a nice car, and the fuel injection was a great improvement, in fact I found there was very little to fault about the driving performance of the Series 3, but my, can they rot! These later cars seem to rust in precisely the same places as earlier XJs, which suggests that Jaguar had learned very little about rustproofing since 1968. My first Series 3 started to rust very quickly, which was most annoying because this was a very expensive car. Nearly every other owner I have spoken to has a similar tale to tell, and indeed it is very unusual to find a rust-

There is a great deal of satisfaction to be gained from a well done paint job . . .

free example. A great pity this, because I consider the Series 3's standards of ride and performance to be the best of all, even though to my eyes its styling can never match the elegance of the Series 2.

Turning now to the XJS, this is a car people either like or loathe. It certainly came as a shock to Jaguar buyers when it was introduced in 1975, its clumsy rear buttresses being the car's most controversial styling feature. Yet despite its visual faults, the design has stood the test of time very well, and few other 20-year-old designs can blend in so well with modern cars as the XJS, which probably has a stronger following today, now that it is no longer in production, than at any time when it was a current model.

I must confess that I fall into the category of those who cannot see anything attractive about the XJS' appearance, although having owned one for a time I am full of admiration for the model's superb mechanics and the wonderful performance it offers. My car came to me not by choice, but as part of a complicated business transaction; it was a case of accepting the Jaguar or losing out on the money I was owed.

This was one of the earlier versions, dating from 1976/77, and it had the rare but desirable manual gearbox. The paintwork was a sort of putty colour and the trim a strange shade of tan. The interior, though comfortable, was not at all Jaguar-like in my opinion, the dashboard and instruments in particular striking me as rather nasty and more in keeping with much lesser cars.

The only work I did on this car was to fit one of the four-headlamp conversion sets, which greatly improved its frontal appearance. Like almost every other Jaguar I have owned, when I took it over it was badly in need of some proper servicing and a thorough cleaning inside, outside and underneath. After I had the car running as it should, its performance I can only describe as exhilarating, and in fact with the manual gearbox it took quite a lot of practice

The only work I did on this car was to fit one of the four-headlamp conversion sets, which greatly improved its frontal appearance.

before I could avoid spinning the wheels during acceleration. It was certainly a most pleasant car to drive, despite the poor rear vision, but being one of the early models its fuel consumption was heavy.

More than once I contemplated a colour change, perhaps to red, but I was never really happy with this car and so I decided instead to look for a new owner for it. This was when I first realized that the car was something of a lemon and would not prove to be very saleable, the manual 'box at that time not being considered a strong selling point.

But I had overlooked two features which in fact made it relatively valuable. The first was that it was still a current model, and the second – and perhaps more important – was that it carried a non-dating number-plate. So when a reputable car dealer pointed this out to me and offered to sell the car on my behalf, guaranteeing me a price I could not believe, I didn't need asking twice. With a few updated items of trim, the XJS looked far younger than its six years, and a happy buyer took it away within two days, the owner of a still-current car in excellent condition for a fraction of its price new.

Looking recently at some advertisements, I am amazed to see high-mileage XJSs for sale at very high prices because I cannot believe that cars which have done 100,000 miles or more can still be of interest to an enthusiast. No matter how often such a car has been serviced, or how many replacement bits have been fitted during its lifetime, it has still done a great deal of hard work, and high mileage tells. A short time ago I drove a three-year-old XJS which had covered around 90,000 miles, and despite its impressive service history and a long list of new parts it still drove like a well used car. Cheap it may have been, but buying a car that has been so extensively used is, I think, buying trouble.

It often baffles me that so many Jaguar buyers will overlook an obvious bargain, yet buy a car that needs a great deal of attention. One XJS I know was on sale locally for more than six months. It was a 10-year-old car, but it was truly immaculate, having had new front wings and a high-quality respray in the original colour. The mechanics were perfect – the gearbox, torque converter, injection system, etc had all been replaced – and the car would have needed nothing spending on it for years barring routine service. It drove just like a Jaguar should, and in the end it sold for less than £2,000 – what a wonderful buy for somebody, and what a contrast with some similar models on sale.

My experience of maintaining the XJS is quite limited, but I must admit that if I were still a committed car renovation enthusiast, even one with good facilities, the XJS would not be a model I would be happy to work on. To begin with, everything seems so complicated, and a lot of the components call for special tools. I have been present at a couple of attempts at home repair by very capable owners, and in both cases I just walked away and left them to it!

Corrosion seems to be quite a problem with these Jaguars, particularly hidden corrosion, and they seem to rot badly in the most unexpected places. One magazine for enthusiasts rebuilt an early example, mainly to illustrate the problems most likely to be encountered, and where, explaining that such an extensive restoration job could never be justified as the car would still be worth less that the cost of the body panels alone. The rebuild of this rusted shell was intended to encourage would-be owners to think very carefully before buying an XJS needing major attention and to remind them that body filler and paint can cover the most unimaginable horrors. That article should be compulsory reading for all buyers of used XJSs.

Looking back...

I have lost count of how many Jaguars have passed through my hands, but I have been left with fond memories of many of them. Of all the models I have owned I think the XJ6 would be my favourite as the best all-rounder for daily use, and my choice of Jaguar purely for pleasure would be an XK150, probably a drophead. It would be impossible to totally dislike any Jaguar, but there have been some that I just could not take a liking to, and this was always because of the model itself, not because I happened to have a poor example of it.

The Mk X must be about the most luxurious of all Jaguars, and a delight to sit in, although it is also said to be the widest Jaguar ever produced. I certainly felt it to be ungainly and cumbersome, so I was never happy to be driving one for long and I was never tempted to buy one. The problem was that it had no sporting pretentions, so it was impossible to have any fun with it. Fast as it was in a straight line, it handled like a barge and the soggy power steering did nothing to help fast cornering. For long motorway trips the Mk X could not be bettered, but as a driver's car it had little to offer me.

Another model I found difficult to like was the S-type, probably because of its strange looks. Head on I thought it looked quite nice, and the rear view was also quite pleasing, but viewed from the side I thought it was awful, as if it were made from Mk X and Mk II leftovers. One part in particular which looked wrong to me was the rear wing, especially the straight-cut bit over the wheelarch. But the interior was superb – far better than the Mk II's – and the independent rear suspension gave a much nicer ride. Yet it never handled as well as the Mk II, or perhaps it was just that I never felt as happy driving one fast as I did a Mk II. I only owned one example, a nice 3.4, which I kept for only a short while, and maybe others felt the same way because the S-type was never a big success and by the early Seventies most of them had disappeared. But possibly even worse, to my eyes, was the rag-bag 420, a sort of miniature Mk X; I'm sure this model was constructed from a parts bin full of leftovers – not a very nice car at all!

My strangest Jaguar was also my oldest – the 2½-litre SS saloon from 1936/37 – the one with the spare wheel in the wing. Somehow it felt very different from other SS saloons I had become familiar with, with a very upright driving position, almost like those of an Austin or

Ford of the period. Suffice to say that when I saw how worn the car had become it was scrapped and I got absolutely nothing for it, such was the worth of SS Jaguars in those days.

Now, of course, the wheel has turned full circle and formerly unloved cars are fetching high prices, although thankfully the ridiculous escalation of perceived values in the late Eighties has since been reversed, hopefully for good. Jaguars, perhaps more than any other make of car, were made to bring enjoyment, and it would be nice to think that the majority of owners still look upon their car, however young or old it may be, as a pleasurable piece of engineering excellence rather than as an investment.

Meanwhile, Jaguars have been the cause of another new hobby – the collection of Jaguar memorabilia – and you can read a lot more about this in the final chapter.

CHAPTER 7

Other Jaguar people

"It's a 'disease' which has afflicted many thousands of us, and one for which there seems to be no cure..."

People who make a habit of running Jaguars can find themselves members of a special type of fraternity, and by that I am not inferring that they all become members of one or other of the officially recognized owners' clubs. It's just that when two or more of them meet, their conversation is invariably steered towards cars – *their* cars. I have lost count of the number of times this has happened to me over the years, and of how many enjoyable hours I have spent comparing notes with fellow Jaguar owners. If nothing else, it has taught me that whatever drew me towards Jaguars in the first place, and then held me there, has been nothing unique – it's a 'disease' which has afflicted many thousands of us, and one for which there seems to be no cure, which of course was precisely what Sir William Lyons intended all along.

In the course of preparing this book I renewed a number of acquaintanceships with people I knew to have been Jaguar owners, and I asked them to recap on their experiences – good and bad – to confirm whether or not they mirrored my own. Some did, and some didn't, but either way, what they had to say I found very interesting. I hope you do, too, because the remainder of this chapter is handed over to them, with my thanks to them for offering us another independent viewpoint on Jaguar ownership.

From Frank Long:
I qualified as an electrical engineer just before the war, so when I came out of the Army I set up in business right away. There were busy factories all over the place and I was lucky to be in demand, designing and installing electrical systems for mass production. Cars were like gold dust in 1946, so I managed with a well-used 1936 Morris 14hp, which drank oil and petrol, but got me around for almost two years. But what I really wanted was an SS Jag, and many were the times that I had sat in the cool desert air of an evening, smoking a Player's and thinking about 'my' car.

About a year after demob, I walked into a showroom in Bolton, Lancashire, one Saturday afternoon. I probably looked a bit grubby after having worked all morning, and I will never forget the snooty look that the salesman gave me. But after signing an order for a new 2½-litre and handing over a £250 cash deposit his change of attitude was amazing. I have never been keen on people like that.

Anyway, about six months passed, then he phoned me one evening to say that a 3½ had suddenly become available and would I be interested? The next afternoon I called to arrange delivery and paid the balance by cheque on the understanding that by the time it had cleared they would have the car available.

It was a black one with brown leather trim – that was quite an attractive shade when new – and I had it taxed for a year and got them to include a full tank of petrol by way of a small discount. At the time we lived in a remote village which was served only by an hourly bus

One Saturday afternoon, I parked my petrol and oil-drinking 1936 Morris 14hp and walked into a showroom in Bolton, Lancashire . . .

The salesman seemed lost for words when I dropped him off at the bus stop and pressed a half-crown into his hand!

Both the Mk VII and the Mk IX covered high mileages, including some continental trips . . .

service. When my 'favourite' salesman insisted on delivering the car personally to me on a Saturday afternoon I made a point of checking over every inch of it before I would accept it – just to be awkward, you understand. No doubt he was expecting me to run him back to the showroom because he seemed lost for words when I dropped him off at the bus stop and pressed a half-crown into his hand!

That weekend I used up a lot of my petrol allowance just driving and driving; we must have done about 300 miles and we enjoyed every minute of it. I had never had a fast car before, but I soon got used to it. In those days the 3½ was one of the fastest cars on the road, and at the time I was having to make a regular trip to South Wales, which meant about 250 miles each way with a stop-over for a couple of nights, and with such little traffic on the roads in those days these trips were a real pleasure. Quite often, though, after I had used up my petrol ration, I would have to use the train for a while.

Those were the days before I had an accountant, so my wife did the books for me, but we were not aware of the tax loopholes that existed for businesses at the time. Consequently, I paid for the Jaguar out of my own money, as well as all the petrol; later on, of course, the business paid for my motoring.

I kept the 3½ until 1953 because I really loved that car and the Mk V simply didn't appeal, so I hung on until I really did have to change to something more modern. I picked up my Mk VII during the month before the Coronation. It was a black car with red trim, not a colour I would have chosen, but this was a cancelled order and the car was being offered at a substantial discount, so I was given a very good deal. By that time the 3½ was exactly six years old, but I have always had my cars serviced regularly so it was in good order. I think I was allowed about £300 for it against the Mk VII.

After that one came a Mk IX, which I liked almost as much as the Mk VII. Both these cars covered high mileages, including some continental trips, and when I put the Mk IX in against a new Mk X it had over 80,000 on the clock, which is the most I have ever done in one car. The reason I hung on to the Mk IX for so long was that I didn't really like the Mk X, in fact I very nearly bought an Alvis instead. But I relented, though the Mk X only stayed with me for about a year because I never really felt happy in it, and then from 1964 to 1968 I ran Mercedes.

But I was happy when the XJ6 came along, and I ordered a 4.2 at once. The car was wonderful, and it never gave me a bit of trouble, but the next one, which I bought three years later, was a different story. It was a typical BL bodge-up – everything went wrong, the car was totally unreliable, it let water in and the body rotted. After that I was off Jaguars again for a while until I bought a later Series 2 4.2, and this one behaved itself, so I kept with Jaguars until after I retired. I usually kept my cars for two years, my last one being a 4-litre Sovereign. Then a couple of years ago I gave up driving. The roads are too crowded now to allow any enjoyment to be had from motoring, and as I was approaching 80 and my eyes were not as good as they used to be I thought it would be safer for all if I started walking.

One of my hobbies has been photography, yet I never took a picture of any of my cars. A short time ago, I was looking through some old papers and realized what those Jaguars had really cost in terms of depreciation, while the money spent on petrol would have kept me in luxury had it been invested! But I have been fortunate enough to have owned 13 new Jaguars and I can honestly say that no other make of car could possibly have given me so much pleasure.

The Aston DB3 disliked town work, but the 1959 Jaguar 3.4 offered all I could have wanted – sportscar performance, a sumptuous interior and good looks.

From Kevin Norris:

When I started to make money, back in the early Sixties, I ran an Aston Martin for a while. It was a DB3 saloon, and the most beautiful car I have ever owned. The exhaust note could crack glass, and I used to drive with the window open whenever I could, just to hear that throaty roar from the tailpipes – wonderful!

The trouble was the Aston disliked town work. It was really more a road-going race car than a car for use in traffic, so I put my lovely car away and bought a 1959 Jaguar 3.4, just to use until I decided what to buy. Well, the 3.4 offered all I could have wanted – sportscar performance, a sumptuous interior and good looks. It was greedy the way I drove it, but luckily buying petrol was no problem. I replaced it early in 1962 with a new Mk II 3.8 and specified white with white leather and chrome wires. In all I had three new Mk IIs, but I never liked any of them as much as my first Mk I.

I ran an E-type for a couple of years, then an XJ V12, a saloon being much more use to me for such things as picking up my hotel customers. As I write this I am using a V12 XJS and have ordered an XJR saloon to replace my 1987 XJ6 3.6, which gave a lot of trouble early in its life but subsequently seemed to settle down. The saloon has done over 70,000 miles now and at times you can taste the fumes, so I would rather offer it in part exchange for the XJR than sell it privately, despite several offers. If the XJR is alright I will probably get rid of the XJS and then use the saloon for pleasure only.

I count myself fortunate in being able to buy any car I want, and I simply like Jaguars because they are so British. A Rolls-Royce or Bentley is just a bit too ostentatious for my taste, and I would not even consider a foreign car.

From Allan Taylor:

My first Jaguar was an E-type roadster, which I bought in 1967 when it was four years old. I had wanted one since they first came out, but I had more important things to concentrate on, like building up my textile business.

Then one day, when the money was coming in and the future looked great, there at the side of the road was this yellow Jag with a 'For Sale' notice on it. I know I should have taken someone along to look at it for me, as I knew so little about them, but after driving it round the block I was hooked. The car seemed to go well and had lots of guts. The seller was an airline pilot, who was just divorced, had sold his house and was going abroad. So as he wanted a quick sale we did a deal there and then and he brought the car round to my house the following evening.

My first surprise was the insurance, which cost about £150, which was a small fortune in those days. Then my wife and I spent an entire day cleaning it inside and out because it was disgusting – like a mobile dustbin. Only then did I realize what a hard life it must have had. There were seven owners in the logbook, the speedo had not worked for ages, the carpets were wet, the oil filler cap had not been off for a long time because it had been cross-threaded, the wipers blew the fuses and there was wheel wobble at speed – any speed, you name it, that car suffered from it.

The E-type looked great standing outside the house and we really enjoyed the short trips we made in it, but I didn't feel happy about going further afield until it had been properly serviced. Then, on the way to the garage, it broke down, right in the middle of the morning rush. What a berk I felt! I walked away and left it for the garage to tow it away.

They kept phoning me at work that day to seek approval for more and more bits. I knew them well, so I knew that the requests would only have been for things that were really needed. Besides all the oils, filters, etc needed for a full service, it required brake pads, wheel bearings, various rubber bushes, electrical parts – the list just went on and on.

The bill came as one hell of a shock, but after all the neglect of the previous owners had been rectified the car was a different creature. I kept it for another year and then I put it in part exchange against a new E-type. From then on I always ran one for as long as they were

I know I should have taken someone along to look at it for me, as I knew so little about them, but after driving it round the block I was hooked.

Leaving the XJS convertible anywhere gave me nightmares after I once found the hood had been cut in an attempt to gain entry.

made and I liked the V12 the best of all.

When the XJS came out I was disgusted because it looked nothing like a Jaguar to me, so I kept my V12 fixed-head until about 1979, when I replaced it with a V12 saloon. Then, when the XJS HE was introduced, I relented and bought one. It was a lovely car to drive, but ugly.

Since then I have kept mainly to saloons, although I did have an XJS convertible for a couple of years. It was a lovely car all round, but leaving it anywhere gave me nightmares after I once found the hood had been cut in an attempt to gain entry.

What I like about the V12 engine is its reserve of power. I travel on the Continent quite often and I can be doing, say, 120mph without any strain, then if I feel like it I can floor the pedal and get up to around the 150mph mark with ease. Most foreign cars have run out of power long before that and nothing much seems to have the stamina of the Jaguar, especially the V12.

I have no mechanical knowledge, so I do nothing to my cars except check the basics. However, I do appreciate fine engineering and I would have no other car. If the day ever came when I could no longer afford a Jaguar, I think I would rather do without a car altogether.

From Charlie Heathcote:
Being a farmer's son, anything mechanical was second nature to me, so before I got a licence I had rebuilt an Austin Seven van ready for taking my test in. After that it was one car after another. I never thought I would have a Jag, though, because only rich people could afford

I noticed a very dirty Mk II Jag right at the back of the lot, and I was taken by it right away.

them, but all that was to change during the cold winter of 1965. That was the time I became hooked on Jaguars.

At the time there were used car lots on wasteland all over Manchester, and one afternoon I stopped by one to look at a Land Rover. It was just a laugh, really, because I already knew Land Rovers inside-out. But this one was polished so well you could have used it for a mirror, and no-one polishes Land Rovers! The tyres had little tread, but there was plenty of boot polish all over them, and a Hoover Diesel badge was fixed to the grille, but the engine looked to me more like it had come from a Trojan Brooke Bond Tea van. The price they were asking took some believing, too.

After a while, the two lads from the pitch came over. They could see I was not a buyer, but they were nice enough blokes. Then I noticed a very dirty Mk II Jag right at the back of the lot, and I was taken by it right away. The body seemed to be very sound around the sills, wheelarches, etc. It was painted in Golden Sand and had tan seats, and apart from flat tyres and a coating of grime several inches thick it looked good. They had bought it in an auction the previous summer, and on the way home the engine had begun to rattle and then had seized.

But it was only five years old and was still a current model, yet the price they wanted was 'a one-er' to take it as seen. They lent me a trolley jack and I was able to see enough of the underside to make my mind up. The exhaust looked new and all the floorpan felt solid, so I paid a small deposit and the next day I went back for the car with a borrowed trailer.

We'd not been married long and my wife went beserk when I told her what I'd spent £100 on, but when she saw the Jag she fell for it at once. She took the bucket of hot water off me and set about cleaning it inside and out, and when she had finished it looked like a two-year-old.

The engine was going to be a problem because I had never worked on anything like a twin-OHC, and reading the manual gave me nightmares. I had also asked about the price of engines, and it began to seem like I had wasted my money. Then I thought about Smithy. We had gone to school together and he had gone on to become a motor mechanic and had set up his own small garage about two years back.

He thought the Jag had been a good buy, and he told me that even with the duff engine he could sell it for a profit. Then he explained what was involved in changing an engine on a 3.4, and a day or so later I managed to take the engine and gearbox out after dropping the suspension.

Lifting the car to pull the engine unit away was no problem because we were well geared up to handle tractors and heavy machines, but the Jag looked sad with no bonnet and its nose up in the air. Smithy helped me strip the engine, which had seized on the crankpins, in fact they had been so hot they were coated in rust. It was as if all the oil had been washed off, and the oil we had drained off the sump was very thin and smelled of petrol. It then occurred to Smithy what had happened: someone, probably at the auction, had 'dosed' the car by pouring petrol in with the oil. This would account for the damage we had found, but of course nothing could ever be proved.

Within a week, Smithy had found me a Mk VII for £15 – it was an MoT failure, but it was still running and complete and had a perfect engine, and the block would fit my 3.4. After doing a spot of work every night, within about two months I had stripped down both engines. Then I checked the Mk VII bottom end and fitted the sump, head, carbs and the other more modern bits from my 3.4, along with a new clutch. The only part I was unable to tackle myself was fitting the head and doing the timing, but putting back the complete engine unit and suspension took a lot longer than the removal.

The new engine fired up almost at once, then Smithy took the car away to tighten everything up, check it over and get it MoT'd, which was the only way I could get him to take any money for all the help he had given me.

After that I used the car whenever I got the chance, and during the Seventies, when Mk IIs

Nothing can take the place of the Mk II for me, but sadly, the Golden Sand 3.4 was written off by a lorry that ran into the back of it.

were being dumped under every hedge, I started collecting spares, then spare cars. I just loved the Mk IIs, both working on them as well as driving them, and there can't be much I haven't done on one, although I have never gone in for rallies or classic car shows, and I have never been a member of an owners' club.

People used to come and pester me for spares, and I'd let them have all sorts for next to nothing, but then I found that when I was stuck for something these same people would want the earth for it, so I thought if that's what fellow enthusiasts are like I'm better off without them.

My wife learned to drive in the 3.4 and used it daily, and later on both my sons learned to enjoy my cars. Although I've tried S-types, XJs and E-types, nothing can take the place of the Mk II for me. Sadly, the Golden Sand 3.4 was written off by a lorry that ran into the back of it. I had just got out of it to go into the bank when this lorry came around the corner and *Bang!* – straight into my Jag. What a mess; it looked as though an express train had hit it, and I'm only glad I wasn't still sitting in it.

People say the strangest things regarding old cars. During the Seventies they would say things like: "Oh, that car's getting on a bit, can't you afford a new one?" Then the other week I was sitting in my current Mk II and this chap came up to me and said: "I bet you're sorry you didn't sell that car a year or so ago when they were fetching big money!" Well, my Jaguars are for my amusement only, and I couldn't give a sod what other people think, although it's nice when I meet people who like the cars in the way I do.

Over the years I've done all sorts of mods to make the cars go faster and make them easier to use in modern traffic. I fitted a 3.8 unit with triple carbs to one car, and that certainly made a difference. The one I have now has an improved axle and gearbox and a modified 4.2 engine with fuel injection. BMW drivers don't like it one bit! We have a Range Rover for use about the farm and a little Astra for day to day use, but it's my special Mk II that gives me the most pleasure.

From Bill Lomas:

I was surprised to discover that my experience with Jaguars would be of any interest to a writer because it seems such recent history. But it was an even bigger surprise to learn that people like myself, who bought new Jaguars and ran them at their personal expense, are in such a minority. You see, I had always had a very good job, but had never qualified for a company car or allowances, so I bought my own and I never thought of doing it any other way.

Just for my own interest, I asked several friends who had enjoyed similar lifestyles and had comparable cars, how their motoring had been financed. Of the nine of us, only one other had ever bought his own cars with his own money. The others had all had company cars, various loans and expenses, or the use of a petrol account. This came as quite a surprise to me, but of course in the Fifties and Sixties no-one admitted having a company car; you would have pretended it was yours. But now, my friends are all retired, like me, and are pleased to boast about how they ran their Jag, or Rover, or Armstrong 'on the firm'.

For most of my working life I travelled by train. I rarely needed a car for work so I kept one for pleasure only. We were married during the war, and I was able to start motoring again within days of my demob. Our first car was bought from a 'friend' and was a Standard Swallow saloon – a pretty looking car, but that is all that could be said for it. During the war it had been laid up, so the wood frame had started to collapse, but I managed to get this patched up so as to keep the car mobile. Someone must have tried to run it on a paraffin

When I lifted the bonnet of the 1½-litre and was confronted with a Standard side-valve engine it brought back memories of the smoky old Swallow.

I fell head over heels for the most beautiful car in the world . . then placed an advert in the evening paper for the Hillman, which brought a queue about a mile long.

mixture at one time because the smell was always present, and it used oil so fast I had to stop every 20 miles or so to top it up. Somehow, I managed with it for 18 months before I was lucky enough to find a very sound Hillman 14hp.

My first Jaguar was very nearly a prewar 1½-litre, but when I lifted the bonnet and was confronted with a Standard side-valve engine it brought back memories of the smoky old Swallow. So we kept the Hillman for four years, and until early 1952 it took us all over the country and had become part of the family. Then, during a day out in the Kent countryside, where we lived, I fell head over heels for the most beautiful car in the world.

It was a red XK120 roadster and was on sale at a garage on behalf of its owner. It was reasonably priced, but it still added up to a lot of money. However, a couple of days later I went on the bus to collect the Jag, then placed an advert in the evening paper for the Hillman, which brought a queue about a mile long.

I kept the XK120 for about five years until we could no longer squeeze our two young children in with us. Being an early model with the alloy body, I had trouble getting rid of it, and in the end it went in part exchange for a year-old Mk VIIM. I felt like I had betrayed a friend when that XK went because she had never failed me, and on the open road she went like a rocket, nothing could get near her.

I kept the Mk VIIM until late 1960, when the new XK150 fixed-head took its place. I enjoyed this car very much, but getting the two kids in the back was not much fun for them; after about 10 miles they were nearly bent double. So I ordered a Mk IX with manual gearbox and individual front seats and took a big loss on the XK150.

I was very annoyed to see the Mk X announced shortly after my Mk IX arrived, and I never really believed the dealer's claimed ignorance of the new model. Of all the Jags, the Mk IX remains my favourite. It was a limousine which could out-perform most sportscars of

I enjoyed the XK150 very much, but getting two kids in the back was not much fun for them.

the time, and I kept it until the summer of 1964, by which time it was looking decidedly old-fashioned.

After thinking long and hard about a replacement, I decided on a Mk X with a manual box and – surprise, surprise – my Jaguar dealer had a couple in stock, though not to the spec I wanted. However, he did find the exact car I wanted within a few days, which tells volumes about how well the Mk Xs were selling.

Then, a couple of months after I had taken delivery, the updated 4.2 version was announced, so this was the second time I had been lumbered with an obsolete car. The Mk X was a wonderful car, but it was very awkward to park. I have heard that they did not corner well at speed, but I was never a reckless driver, so I never encountered that problem.

My only accident happened whilst I was driving that 3.8 Mk X. I had been to London by train and had left the car in the car park of a long since demolished station where I used to catch the express. Returning in the evening a few days later, I was pleased to find the car undamaged, but it was not to remain so for long. As I waited at a red light on the main road a double-deck bus came flying out of a side street, right towards my car, and there was nothing I could do. At the last moment the driver swerved and braked, but the back end of the Jag took the full impact, and I was knocked sideways.

Luckily I was unhurt, but the car was a write-off, as was my luggage in the boot. But the outcome was a happy one because, after my lawyers had finished their discussions with the bus' insurers, sufficient funds were made available to provide me with a new C-registered 4.2 Mk X.

Starting with that Mk X, which I bought in 1965, I usually changed my cars after about two years, but when the XJ6 was first made I wasn't very keen on it. So I bought a new 420G in 1971, which was one of the very last made, and I kept it for nearly three years. The

A double-deck bus came flying out of a side street . . . the 3.8 Mk X was a write-off, as was my luggage in the boot, but there was a happy outcome – the insurers paid for a new 4.2!

Jaguars have given me much to be grateful for, and more pleasure than almost anything in the world.

replacement was a Series 2 XJ6 4.2; I liked the look of these much more than the earlier cars.

Ever since, I have kept with XJ saloons, always with the biggest engine option. The only one I was never too happy with was a 3.6, an early Series 4 from around 1987. The build quality of this particular car was very poor, the electrics kept playing up and I was forever irritated by things coming loose, squeaks, rattles and damp carpets.

The only other Jaguar that gave me cause for complaint was a Series 3, which showed rust spots very early in its life. Funnily enough, I saw the car again in 1991, by which time it was eight years old and the body was in a terrible state.

After much thought I have recently ordered a 4-litre Sovereign, and it will probably be my last. Now that I am retired I like a peaceful life, and even going to the shops can be such a bind with cars everywhere and nowhere to park, so quite often we take a taxi.

But I have always loved driving, and even when the roads started to get really congested, driving a Jaguar was still a pleasure. Somehow, you feel so safe and secure sitting in one, insulated from the world outside and all its pressures. Many is the time I have sat in the car, parked on the front drive, enjoyed a cigaratte and let my troubles just drift away. In fact Jaguars have given me much to be grateful for, and more pleasure than almost anything in the world.

From Dave Watkin:
Late in 1961 I started work as an apprentice motor mechanic at a Jaguar main dealer. They were a good firm to work for, and they gave me a day off each week to go to college. It was all Mk IIs then – not many of the big saloons came in, although there were quite a few 150s, and later on of course the E-type. They were a very popular car, and we seemed to handle more of them than we did the saloons.

We young lads used to fight to drive them from the car park round to the workshop, but the firm wouldn't even let you drive a car in the 'shop until you had passed your test. Road tests were the older mechanics' perks, and we were limited to taking a car around the block for a brake test.

The compound held lots of older cars that had been taken in part-exchange, and things like Mk VIIs and XKs were left to rot after being plundered for bits. As the firm is no longer in business I don't mind saying now that many an owner of a new car needing components replaced under warranty would have driven away happily, unaware that his problem had been solved with some not so new parts! We all had XK badges and chrome Jaguar words all over our toolboxes, and most of the lads did 'foreigners' and helped themselves to bits from the old car stock as no-one seemed to bother.

I specialized on engines, and at one time E-types were having a lot of valve problems, but I could have a head off, on the bench and stripped before it had cooled down. Setting valve clearances was the worst job, but that apart the OHC engines were a cinch to work on. After a while, I could set a three-carb engine up by feel, and the timing, too, as well as the Sun tuner we had. Gearboxes were easy to repair, and the old Moss 'box was like something out of a tractor. It was just like doing Meccano, whereas the later all-synchro 'boxes were a bit more fiddly, though I soon got used to them.

I managed to get good qualifications and I progressed into management, but the motor trade was becoming soulless; cars were being talked about as volume of new units, and unrealistic targets were being set for both the salesmen and the workshop staff. The accountants had taken over and the atmosphere had gone; the funny thing is the old firm only lasted a few years under this new regime before the liquidators came in.

A year or so before that, I had decided I wanted no more of this constant pressure, and my wife and I took over the Free House that we still have today. We run it as a traditional pub, the sort of place we would like to visit ourselves, and the policy works. We attract just enough of the right sort of people, and we contract out the catering, so we don't need to worry about that. The pub has no sign of my motoring past, but instead is devoted to my

. . . he threw me the logbook. "Here, you can have the bugger," was all he said.

lifelong passion for steam railways, with station signs and railway relics filling most of the rooms.

My very first Jaguar – this would be around 1967 – was a 1951 3½-litre Mk V. It appeared on the compound one weekend and it was obvious that it had been stored for ages. Monday dinner time and I was all over it. The mileage was less than 30,000, the car had been looked after, and on the screen was its last tax disc, dating from 1961. It was metallic grey with red trim, the battery was dead flat, but the engine fired up readily enough when I got a charge to it.

The sales manager had the say about where all the used cars went, so I told him I wanted to do the Mk V up properly and use it myself. He stared at me blankly for a moment, then after a quick rummage amongst the papers on his desk he threw me the logbook. "Here, you can have the bugger," was all he said. As I said, the firm was very easy-going.

The Mk V had a thorough going-over, a proper service and a clean-up, all out of working hours, and I drove it home with a current and quite 'straight' MoT. The car was in daily use until I got married in 1970 and it was one of the nicest Jaguars I have ever owned. But they were worth very little at the time, and when I sold it I think I got about £35 for it with tax and MoT.

After a couple of years with smaller cars I went back to Jaguars, which I could always buy cheaply; running them was always the big expense. The compact saloons were my favourite, and for quite a while I ran a 3.8 S; it was about four years old when I got it, and my only complaint was that it drank oil. After that I had Mk IIs – always the bigger ones – and for a short time a 420, although this was a car I could never get to like. After promotion I ran a company car, but sadly it was not a Jaguar, so for about five years, until we got the pub, I was without one.

I took the V12 on what was probably its first motorway trip, let it get warm for a few miles, then opened her up; the filth came flying out of the pipes, clouds of it, then suddenly there was a clean exhaust.

Then a retired chap I'd known since my apprentice days offered me his V12 saloon at a price I couldn't refuse. It was nearly four years old, but it had done less than 6,000 miles – all short trips from home to the golf club, home to the shops and into town once a week to visit the bank and fill the tanks up. He had decided to give up driving and let his wife run him around. The V12 must hardly have got warm and it just wouldn't run smoothly. A garage had told him that it wanted a decoke and a new injection system.

At first I thought the car had a dose of the dreaded black sludge, but flushing the engine a couple of times resulted in clean oil. Then I overhauled the fuel injection myself, and Wow!, what a difference. The combustion chambers were obviously well coked-up, but I cleared that easily enough, one of my trade secrets being a liquid for shifting carbon – just add it to the fuel, let it work its way around, and the dirt just comes flying out.

I took the V12 on what was probably its first motorway trip, let it get warm for a few miles, then opened her up; the filth came flying out of the pipes, clouds of it, and then suddenly there was a clean exhaust. After that the car was a dream to drive. I kept it for a couple of years and then traded it in against a 4.2; I missed the V12, but it had been very, very greedy.

Nowadays, I buy a car which is about a year old and keep it for a further two years. It's my own money, so this way I can keep depreciation to a minimum. I've still got contacts in the trade, so I am lucky to be able to choose nice used Jaguars at very fair prices.

These days I rarely handle tools, and an ex-fellow apprentice, who now runs a garage, does all my servicing, etc. The only time I get dirty finger nails now is when I put in a day at our steam centre; being a mechanic is a clean job compared with that!

The last work I did on a Jag was over two years ago. A mate had bought an XK140 with a tired engine and I rebuilt it for him after having the crank done, the block rebored, reworked the head, and stripped, checked and modified the gearbox. I really enjoyed doing that, and later on my test run in the car, but I try to keep quiet about my background; the worst thing you can do in a pub is to let people think you know all about cars – I've got enough customers like that!

My present car is a 4-litre Jaguar Sovereign, which was 18 months old when I bought it with 26,000 miles up. I think that's a lot of work for such a short time, but the car runs well, and if I keep it two years I will probably take the total to around 45,000.

To me, nothing can offer the same value as a Jaguar, and I think that in order to get the same degree of performance and comfort as the present models offer you have to be looking at a Rolls or a Bentley. No other make of car would even tempt me, at least not for regular use, although I will admit that if a nice Aston Martin came along I would be very tempted....

"Now, how can I have been doing 80 miles an hour.. ..when I've only been out 10 minutes?"

It's been tried, it really has . . . but I doubt whether it's ever worked!

CHAPTER 8

Interior restoration

"Today, a vast range of materials and services are available to the enthusiast intent on improving a Jaguar's interior."

I remember quite clearly the first time I undertook some major restoration of a Jaguar interior. The car was an SS-type saloon, which badly needed a new headlining, and I faced serious problems in obtaining a replacement. Jaguar agents had long ago cleared their stocks of such items, and the only firm of hood makers and trimmers in the area had quoted me a price which exceeded the value of the car.

But to the rescue came the little textile firm that had supplied the material for the new wool headlining, and a few days after delivering to them the carefully removed but fragile original I collected a beautifully made replacement in grey wool fabric.

I seem to recall that fitting this was quite fiddly, to say the least. As far as I remember, the material was held in place by tacks along both sides, which meant constant adjustment to get all the creases out. The lining was held in place at the back by the inner chrome frame of the rear window, and at the front it was tucked under the wood screen surround.

The edges were disguised by a panel containing the interior lights, which also formed a sort of side headrest for rear seat passengers. These panels narrowed off just above the back doors, and from that point to the front of the screen a long narrow strip was fixed to what Jaguar describe as the cantrail. Trimming and then fixing these trim panels was probably the worst part of the whole job, but it was more than worth the effort.

Today, a vast range of materials and services are available to the enthusiast intent on improving a Jaguar's interior, but there are still many pitfalls for the unwary. Of course, sumptuous interiors are only a part of the Jaguar magic, but shabby trim can spoil the appeal of an otherwise well kept and restored car, and improvement to an acceptable standard can be achieved at a reasonable cost.

Whilst most enthusiasts tend to be very capable and adaptable, some aspects of interior renovation are best left to the professionals, or only undertaken after very careful thought. Restoration of woodwork is one task that even the most skilled enthusiast should be very wary of because although excellent results can be obtained by patience and practice, mistakes, even minor ones, can be very costly indeed.

Most Jaguar woodwork is veneer on ply. Some sources say that Jaguar used matched veneer (wood from the same tree) for the sets of wood for each car, but others disagree, saying that veneer with a similar grain was often acceptable, and in such cases dyes were used to give a uniform colour after lacquering. Often, after stripping, sets of wood will have veneers of quite different shades, which does tend to confirm this theory.

Incidentally, the numbers found in chalk or crayon on the back of many wood sets refer to a set matched to a car and not necessarily to the veneers having been carefully selected. Remember, Jaguar were always working to a price, so waste was never tolerated to the same extent that others might have allowed. Because of this, stopper or grain filler will often be found after stripping veneer. Again this was to avoid waste and, after all, it's a method

In many respects, interior work is the most critical part of Jaguar restoration, requiring both skill and patience in abundance. For this reason, it is also often the most neglected part, though not in this instance!

Upholstery renovation means more than merely restoring the worn surfaces. Of equal importance – for reasons of comfort as well as appearance – is the investigation and rectification of any causes of sagging prior to refinishing.

Perfectly aligned and presented seatbacks. The three views on this and the previous page are of a Mk II saloon after it has undergone treatment from A & B Leather Renovations, John Sundberg's specialist re-dyeing and trimming business in Coggeshall, Essex.

accepted by cabinetmakers and in no way should it detract from a well finished surface. The high gloss was achieved by sprayed on lacquer, cellulose-based, although I believe that synthetic products were in use at least some of the time. Sadly, these lacquers could not stand up to our British climate for long, dampness being their worst enemy, which caused the lacquer to crack and flake.

Despite not having done any restoration work for a number of years, and therefore being hopelessly out of practice, I recently had some remarkable results restoring a Mk II dash top that had been in the garage for many years. Having been exposed to damp at some time, not only was the lacquer lifting, so was the veneer. I began by using a water-washable stripper to remove the lacquer. Fine wire wool is a great help to ensure that all traces of the lacquer are removed, and it will not damage the surface. Water-washable stripper is a 'must' in my opinion as the solvents used to neutralize other strippers can not only discolour the veneer, but can also dissolve the glue.

Where the veneer had lifted I reglued it in place using a woodworking glue which is a household name. I also took the opportunity to replace bits of missing veneer, not with any hope of getting a perfect match, but more to see how neat a job could be made of 'piecing in'. The best results were obtained by placing a piece of new veneer on top of the damaged area, then cutting through both pieces together. It is somewhat tricky holding the new bit in place whilst wielding a sharp knife, but with a little practice an excellent fit can be obtained.

I found that wetting the new piece helped greatly with the cutting, and I discovered that there was no alteration in size after drying. Also, the new piece can be held in place with masking tape before cutting through both tape and veneer. To begin with I really struggled to glue such small pieces in place, but then in desperation I tried another method, which really worked. This is the procedure:

Firstly, ensure that the new piece is a perfect fit, although of course if it overlaps any edges

Badly discoloured seating from an S-type Jaguar with cracking and other obvious signs of wear.

The S-type's seats after the application of A & B's re-dying process.

An example of veneer which has been damaged due to a combination of water and sunlight.

can be trimmed later. Then, if the piece has dried out, dampen it again, apply adhesive to both pieces and allow to dry. When the glue is fully dry, pop the new piece in place and reactivate the glue using a hot iron. Using a smoothing iron in this way helps greatly with adhesion to curved surfaces, and I am convinced that it also seals the pores of the veneer, helping the polishing process.

After trimming the new piece I smoothed the whole surface by hand, using very fine sandpaper, and finished off with some well worn paper. It is important to be careful not to rub through the veneer, particularly at the edges and joints, where it will be very thin. Final preparation with smooth, worn paper will ensure a smooth surface free of scratches. Remember that preparing veneer is a little like preparing metal for painting in that every scratch and blemish, however slight, will be horribly magnified by the application of the finishing material.

The veneer on my dash top was very pale after stripping and it had a few blemishes, mostly where the little knots had parted company with the veneer, and the joints on some of my repairs needed tidying. For this I used a commercial stopper of the type used by french polishers, which is readily available.

With a well-prepared surface, I decided to experiment by trying three different finishes. On one of the parts where I had done my repairs I used a wood dye to give a much darker colour, another part was given a coat of french polish, whilst the remaining part was to have just the lacquer applied. The lacquer I used was a modern acrylic-based product as it had to be applied by spray gun at quite high pressure; I had to get someone to coat my wood for me.

The results were excellent. The material dried quickly and gave a wonderful mirror-like gloss. However, having been present at the time, I must say I would recommend that such products are used only by professionals with suitable extraction equipment.

A dashboard top which has been previously worked on and ruined by over-zealous stripping of the old laquer. The only solution was to re-veneer.

My repairs had blended in very well, in spite of making no attempt to match the veneer. The stain had not hidden the grain and had given the wood a lovely colour. The part I had french polished looked the best, the polish having really highlighted the grain, but even the pale veneer looked very nice. So here were three excellent finishes, achieved with simple variations in preparation, which just went to indicate what an expert might have achieved with modern materials.

I should mention that some of these new lacquers are so good that no strippers appear to be available to remove them. The makers of one of them apparently can see no valid reason why the product should ever need to be removed, presumably being unaware of the results of Jaguar dashboards expanding or contracting in extreme temperatures. I know that as I write this a chemical company is working on such a stripper, but in the meantime the permanence of these products does give cause for some concern.

The excellent results I obtained should have been good enough for any enthusiast other than those preparing their car to *concours* standard. However, for anyone lacking patience, or being unhappy at handling materials – and in some cases equipment – which do require special care, my advice would be to leave this work to a professional, some of whom offer special rates to Jaguar owners.

Complicated veneering is a job I would definitely leave to the experts because the materials are expensive and difficult to work with. Having said that, most capable enthusiasts could, I feel sure, do a wonderful job of veneering and polishing a small flat surface, but something like a Mk IX dashboard could spell disaster. Imagine having to veneer the bevelled edges of the speedo and rev-counter holes, having to butt-join two sheets of veneer and match the grain, cut holes for switches and the like, when one simple mistake could mean having to strip the whole lot off and start again. Enjoyable and satisfying as the work can be, I would recommend the services of a professional wood restorer, whose results should be well worth paying for.

I have already mentioned my experience of replacing the headlining of the SS saloon, but I have also performed a similar job on Mk VII and Mk II Jaguars, in both cases using original Jaguar components. This is a part of an older Jaguar that all too often requires attention because a tatty headlining can spoil the appearance of an otherwise tidy car. Usually the problem has been caused by smoking or the effects of dampness due to leaking window rubbers.

In the main, Jaguar headlinings have been of wool or a wool mix material, and all too often an attempt at cleaning such material results in staining and sagging. Therefore, the only wise thing to do with an old and shabby headlining is to replace it. These days, specialized companies can supply headlinings for nearly every Jaguar model, sometimes in kit form, and as I have indicated, fitting one is not particularly difficult, just fiddly and time-consuming. The main requirements are patience and very clean hands.

Don't be surprised to reveal a very rusty roof, and do consider replacing screen rubbers if there is the slightest sign of water getting in. In the case of my Mk II, it had the common problem of a leaking rear window, and the sight of stained cloth in my rear-view mirror annoyed me so much that within a week of buying the car I had started work on replacing the headlining.

The job was made a little easier because I removed the rear screen rubbers at the same time. However, there is a lot of trim to remove on the Mk II, and I seem to remember that in this instance it was all a bit of a struggle. The lining itself on this car is fixed by metal rods running from side to side and is glued or tacked at the edges and at front and rear. The rods hold the headlining taut and stop sagging, but great care is needed to eliminate all the creases before fixing the edges. I doubt whether I would ever tackle another Mk II myself as I recall having to struggle to get all the creases out, and even then I was never totally happy with the result.

The Mk VII was much easier, probably due to the sheer size of the car, which meant that there was plenty of room to move around inside. The car, which belonged to a friend, was in wonderful condition except that its previous owner had decided to brighten up the headlining by giving it a coat of white emulsion. The result was awful – it was a ghastly bright white, and the paint having made the cloth shrink, it was now as tight as a drum skin. To the artist's credit, though, there was not a speck of emulsion on the seats, the carpets or the woodwork.

Even with a lot of trim and a sunroof to remove, the transformation of the Mk VII did not present much difficulty. Although all this happened a long time ago, the only problem I recall was in fitting the lining around the sunroof opening without creases.

Door panels and other bits of interior trim are mainly a matter of common sense, and quite often wonderful improvements can be made with a little imagination and ingenuity. Apart from wear and tear, the most common problems are discolouration and the rotting away of the backing boards. Most of these backing boards are hardboard, but many of the earlier cars used thin plywood.

Leather trim can often be restored using the same type of materials as are available for cleaning and dying seats. Vinyl trim not only discolours, but can also become misshapen over the years. Some people have used vinyl paints in an attempt to restore panels, but personally I think such paints make a disgusting mess. However, I have seen much worse things used to paint panels, and even seats!

Replacement backing boards, and even complete panels, are available for some cars, but if you have to make your own boards for door or other interior panels, it is not particularly difficult, although cutting the holes for window winders, trim clips, etc can be awkward and very time-consuming. I used to have a set of hole cutters for leather – the sort of giant punches as used by saddlers, etc – and such items are surely still available from craft suppliers.

Preparing a Mk II dashtop for re-veneering. Imperfections in the base wood must be filled and smoothed before fixing the new veneer so as to ensure there are no air bubbles or dips in the finished job.

Having got your new boards, it is certainly worth making some attempt to protect them from damp, so if you have the patience, paint around all the edges – any sort of paint will do – so as to protect these vulnerable places from acting like a sponge, because hardboard and ply can soak up water at a rapid rate. Fortunately, given the huge range of trim products on offer today, it is often possible to restore your own panels to a professional standard at a very low cost.

There is very little that can be done with worn carpets other than to replace them. However, should you have one of those vacuum cleaners that doubles as a carpet cleaner you can often make an amazing difference to dirty, grubby carpets. A word of warning: do be very careful when buying carpet sets for a Jaguar, especially if you are buying them by mail order. Deal with a reputable company, preferably one that has been recommended, and certainly one that will give you a full refund should you not be satisfied. Jaguar carpets were of good quality and made to high standards, so anything less will only serve to make the car look tacky.

Many years ago I sent for a fitted black carpet set for an E-type, and it was not cheap. But when it arrived I just couldn't believe what rubbish it was. It had been made from a series of nylon tufts, which had been glued to thin sacking, backed with polythene. I would not have used it in a dog's basket, let alone a Jaguar, and in the end I got my money back, though not without some difficulty. These same people were still advertising 'original-spec carpets' quite recently!

Surely there cannot be many Jaguars over 20 years old which still have their original, unrestored leather seats. Well, it seems there must be , for Jaguar seats appear to have been made of strong stuff. Despite years of neglect, many leather seats have survived quite well. The main signs of wear tend to be scuffs and tears, and split seams due to rotted stitches, and all of these and even worse faults can be rectified to a very acceptable standard. Again, all

that is needed is a little patience, and the help of some of the excellent user-friendly products that are now available to the enthusiast.

Ideally, leather seats should be cleaned once a year, using a proper leather cleaner, not water, which will only harden the leather and, in time, rot the stitches. The surfaces should be fed on a regular basis as proper hide food penetrates the leather, making it supple, and therefore less prone to splits and cracks. But how many leather-upholstered cars have received such treatment, I wonder?

Motor accessory shops are stacked with products claiming to clean and restore all types of upholstery, and a lot of these are most expensive. For vinyl seats and trim, some of them are fine, but the effects of using them on leather could be, to say the least, questionable. I have always used leather cleaners and hide foods sold to treat saddlery and furniture and have obtained excellent results from them. But recently I came across a leather cleaner and a hide food which had been developed specifically for treating car upholstery, and I must admit I have found the results to be far superior to anything I have used previously. The leather cleaner, which gives excellent results quickly, is used to prepare surfaces for application of the hide food. It is recommended that the liquid leather food is rubbed gently into the surface and allowed to penetrate. Ideally, it should be left for several days to soak in before buffing. The hide certainly becomes more supple, and even looks and smells better, so it is an excellent treatment for 'tired' leather and a most pleasant product to use.

Several years ago, I tried out a leather dyeing kit on the seats of a Mk II Jaguar, and I must say that I quite enjoyed the task. Taking out all the seats, cleaning and preparing them properly, and following instructions to the letter, my intention was to restore the seats to their original colour – just that. The overall appearance was wonderful, but I was never happy with the result because the colour was not even and it failed to cover the areas that had scuffed or creased. But worst of all, the dye was never fast, so it kept staining people's

Examples of Mk II door capping both before and after re-lacquering.

clothes, and in the end I fitted seat covers and made the best of a bad job. Needless to say, after that I had very little faith in leather renovation kits, in any form.

Therefore, it was a pleasant experience to come across a leather redye kit that gives good results. Using this material requires considerable patience and care, careful preparation of the leather being most important. Before doing anything, though, I would advise removing the seats from the car and examining the leather carefully to see if it has been treated in the past. It is surprising what people will use to try to smarten up leather seats, even paint, although some other coatings are not quite so obvious.

All remains of earlier treatments must be removed completely, and if you are in doubt as to what you are trying to remove, you will need to resort to cellulose thinners. This will not harm the leather as it tends to evaporate quickly. Also, the use of fine wire wool will do the surface no harm if used with care.

However, do be prepared for a nasty gooey mess when using thinners. Not only will it dissolve whatever the seats have been treated with, but often the original dye as well. This stage calls for plenty of clean rags and a lot of hard work. Afterwards, the leather must be washed thoroughly with soap and hot water, then properly rinsed off and allowed to dry naturally. This can often take 24 hours or more, depending on conditions.

At this stage I would be investigating such repairs as needed doing. The leather covers are not difficult to take off, you just need to remember what fitted which way and exactly where all the clips went when the time comes to put it all back together again.

Quite often, broken stitching can be repaired with not too much difficulty, but if the stitches have torn through the leather you may have problems that only a new section can cure. Whatever you do, don't try to force a needle through hard leather; soak the area you intend to stitch before you begin as that way you will avoid tearing the needle holes. Then investigate any causes of sagging – it may be simply broken up foam, but it could be

A picture which shows clearly how the colour of the door panel has faded due to sunlight. The part which has been covered by the door capping retains its darker original colour.

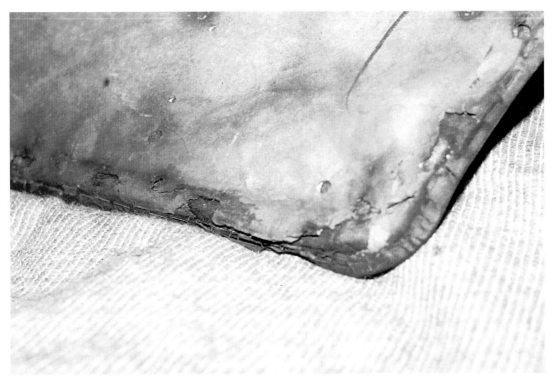

The back of a door panel showing how prolonged dampness has ruined the board

something more serious such as broken springs or a part of the frame. At this stage it is well worth delaying the redyeing operation in order to do a little remedial work. Also, it can sometimes be helpful to utilize a seat squab from another car so as to make sure that the colour match of the dye will be acceptable

Now, using the redye kit to which I have already referred, it is time to clean the surface to be dyed with a special cleaner mixed with hot water. This should be done regardless of whatever cleaning you may already have carried out as it also conditions the leather for the subsequent work. An excellent sealer is provided for application by spraygun at quite high pressure. The manufacturers suggest an initial application by brush to areas where cracks and creases are present as this will give added coverage and a better finish. For leather that is heavily cracked or creased an all-over brushed-on coat is recommended. Then, when the seats are touch-dry, which will probably be after a couple of hours, the final coat of suitably thinned resin dye can be applied by spray.

Although touch-dry within hours, the treated surfaces must be left to dry properly for a week, after which the hide food should be applied. Provided the instructions have been followed, the seats should now be redyed to a uniform colour and made to look as original as the condition of the leather will allow. Do not expect a miracle one-coat cure from a bottle to make worn and 'tired' leather like new (apparently some people do!), but the results obtainable from the kit I tested, which was selling for about £40, should be entirely acceptable to most people.

However, for the perfectionist, only a retrim may be good enough, the cost of which in all probability would exceed the value of the car in need of restoration. Full leather trim kits, designed for DIY enthusiasts, are now made to such high standards that it would be impossible to tell that such a kit was not the work of a professional trimmer. Also, help and advice is available to the enthusiast from the suppliers of such kits to ensure that the desired end result is achieved. When you learn that a kit for a Mk II costs around £2,000, you can only imagine what the cost of a full retrim would be.

As an enthusiast whose main enjoyment has always been working on and improving – rather than driving or exhibiting – cars, I am delighted to see such a large number of new and innovative products available today. Interior restoration has turned full-circle since I renewed the headlining of my SS in the early Sixties. There was little choice then but to have a go yourself, but later, when restoration became the norm, specialists sprang up everywhere willing to renovate your interior, so long as you could pay. The past few years have seen a vast new range of versatile and reasonably priced materials which have been developed to enable enthusiasts to achieve standards of excellence in interior restoration that could not have been possible only 10 years ago.

Some of the methods I have described in this chapter are merely my personal preferences – the best ways for me to get the results I was aiming for – so it is quite likely that craftsmen or other enthusiasts more experienced than myself might not necessarily agree with me. Also, I have chosen not to recommend, or even to name, some of the well known products I have used – I think it is fairer that way. However, I cannot close without offering my very special thanks to John Sundberg, of A&B Leather Restorations – a fellow Jaguar enthusiast – for all his help and advice on this subject.

Jaguar automobilia

"Anything and everything Jaguar-related, it seems, is of interest to a collector somewhere...."

Like thousands of other enthusiasts worldwide, I could never resist picking up various bits and pieces to do with old cars. In my case, the disease in the main has been limited to things related to Jaguars, and it really began by salvaging small items lying around in scrapyards. A radiator badge, some instruments, perhaps a handbook or some tools, just small but interesting items that would otherwise have been burned or destroyed. Most of the Jaguar items seemed to have an appeal one way or another, probably because of the quality of their design or styling, and even an early SS wheel spinner found a use as a doorstop and became quite an attraction to visitors.

Then, a few years ago, a new magazine appeared, which was aimed specifically at people like me. Through *Jaguar Automobilia Collector* I discovered not only that my hobby had a name, but also that there were thousands of others around the world who shared my interest. I am indebted to Ian Cooling, the magazine's dedicated editor, not only for agreeing to read this chapter in draft form, but also for correcting a few errors which had crept in and adding some invaluable additional information and comments, which have now been incorporated.

Nowadays, almost anything Jaguar-related seems to be very highly collectable, so much so that all the major auction houses include Jaguar items in their sales. Not so long ago, commonplace items such as mascots from the Sixties and Corgi toys were fetching hugely inflated prices, but fortunately values have settled of late to a more reasonable level.

Although the auctioneers have jumped on the gravy train, many Jaguar items are still available at sensible prices if you know where to look. But sadly, a lot of reproductions have appeared on the market, some of them so cleverly aged as to deceive not only the inexperienced. I know at least one experienced collector who has paid dearly for an item he believes to be the real thing, and perhaps it is better if he never discovers the truth.

So what do people collect? Well, in the case of one person I know it's engines – every possible variation of the Jaguar twin-OHC engine, including the rare 2-litre version. Each engine is attached to a gearbox and after cleaning and painting has been mounted on a purpose-built tubular frame. Every one is complete with auxiliaries, just as it would have been when it left the factory.

Another enthusiast, again someone to whom storage is not a problem, collects absolutely anything that takes his fancy – rolling chassis, body panels, even a couple of complete bodyshells, both of them brand new. The rest of us, however, have to limit ourselves to items which need a little less space, and one of the most popular subjects is collecting sales brochures.

All such material is in constant demand, from the earliest known SS1 and SS2 folders, *circa* 1931, to the most up-to-date. I have found nearly all SS and Jaguar literature to be most pleasing to the eye as well as very descriptive, the presentation invariably being superb,

A silver-mounted perpetual calendar with the SS wings badge top centre. The silver plaque on the wooden base is engraved with the recipient's name. These pieces were given to dealers and blue-chip customers as well as to senior staff as gifts on retirement or similar auspicious occasions. (*Ian Cooling Collection*)

often with full-colour artwork of cars, interiors and even mechanical details. Ian Cooling, though, has a valid comment to make about this: "While I would generally agree with this, I think there are a group of brochures from the period when Jaguar was almost submerged within British Leyland, which share the generally bland and uninspiring design of that organization's publicity department. To my mind, the best years were from about 1935 to 1940, and the past six years or so, when the influence and pennies of Ford have begun to make an impact. I have in mind such recent brochures as the XJ220 and the XJR-S, as well as those superbly designed 'folder' brochures in heavy British Racing Green card from a couple of years ago."

When I left school in the early Sixties such items were readily available for just a few coppers. One particular secondhand bookshop had a vast collection of unused car brochures at sixpence or a shilling each. I think I must have bought most of the SS and Jaguar ones at that time, but sadly I didn't keep them.

Expert knowledge is needed to operate in this complex area. For example, I believe that about 25 basic SS brochures were issued, and that excludes reprints, etc. Postwar material offers even more confusion and variation, and that is before you even start to think about prices. So anyone thinking about collecting Jaguar brochures would be wise to befriend an experienced collector or two before trawling the autojumbles with cheque book at the ready.

The modern laser copiers can produce some high-quality copies of rare brochures, although as Ian Cooling points out, even the best of them is unlikely to produce colour reproduction of a quality high enough to deceive even the non-specialist eye. "However, your general point is spot-on as there are other printing techniques available in quite small printing houses able to produce copies of such as the C-type and D-type folders which are virtually indistinguishable from the originals. In my experience, it is usually the paper that

Right, a mint prewar mascot mounted on a presentation ashtray and, immediately below it, an unusual presentation piece with merry times in mind! The mascot is cast in bronze with a walnut veneered base which contains a small partitioned drawer. The mascot lifts off the base and a corkscrew spiral (contained in the drawer) is fitted into a hole in its stomach. The elongated upper lip of the mascot also serves as a bottle-opener! (*Ian Cooling Collection*)

Below, a prewar mascot mounted on a Mk IV radiator cap. The mascot clearly shows pitting of the chrome plating – probably the combined result of weathering and a chemical reaction between the casting alloy and the plate. (*Ian Cooling Collection*)

Handbooks spanning 60 years from the early 1930s (top left) to the early 1990s (bottom centre). The large D-type handbook in the centre is especially rare. (*Ian Cooling Collection*)

gives the game away rather than the printing. But this presupposes that you have a genuine and guaranteed original handy for comparison!"

Handbooks and service manuals, too, have become very collectable, for like the sales brochures, they are well-prepared and presented and also make good reading. Prewar material in good condition is very scarce, as are books covering the first postwar cars. Handbooks for all models from the mid-Fifties still seem to be plentiful, although certain versions are more in demand than others.

Workshop manuals are easy to get to grips with. For example, there would be a manual for the Mk I saloon in basic form, then supplements to cover the various mods and spec changes. But handbooks are far more complex. A few are dated, but revised handbooks were printed to cover mods or production changes. Most postwar handbooks have a publication code, but it needs an expert to decipher them.

The potential for anyone wishing to collect handbooks must be almost unlimited. Whilst I know of no official list of all the variations, it is said that there are at least four versions of most Jaguar handbooks issued since 1946. Indeed, my informant, a well-established collector, has no less than 11 different versions for the 1½-litre model (and Ian Cooling can beat him with 13 and he knows of three others!), plus five for the 3.8 and about nine for the E-type, and he knows his collection is not complete. However, as Ian Cooling pointed out to me, there are also certain limited-run handbooks, such as those for the D-type, the XJ coupe and the XJ 220, for which there has been only one edition. "Also, although there were a large number of different handbooks for the XJ series, quite a few of the individual variations had less than four editions. I particularly have in mind the AKM series of handbooks."

Car salesmen from the earliest days must have been pestered by souvenir-hunters, and SS and Jaguar salesmen must have suffered more than most. All showroom or garage items to

A sumptuous prewar catalogue. Cord-bound, the heavily embossed thick card cover is mounted with a very elegant gold and green metallic logo. (*Ian Cooling Collection*)

Little and large! The 1940 range brochure (left) alongside its tiny equivalent produced in 1945 to comply with postwar paper rationing. (*Ian Cooling Collection*)

do with Jaguar are in great demand, and once again the company have produced some lovely items over the years.

Apart from posters, photos, display material, wall signs, etc, SS and Jaguar dealers were often presented with such items as tea trays, cigarette boxes, ashtrays and various desk ornaments, all of which were decorated with the appropriate logo. Many such items, of course, found their way into private homes and probably never adorned an office desk.

One of my more recent finds was an XK140 grille badge mounted on an alloy disc to act

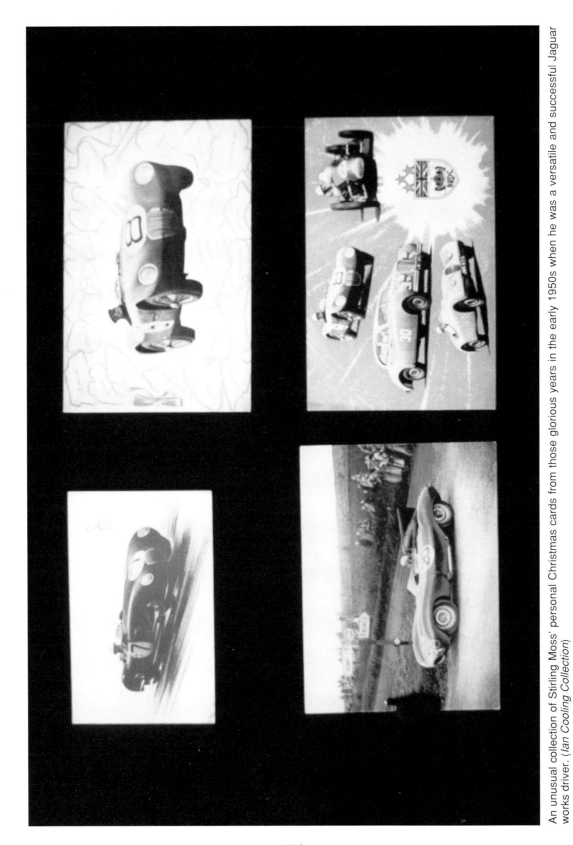

An unusual collection of Stirling Moss' personal Christmas cards from those glorious years in the early 1950s when he was a versatile and successful Jaguar works driver. (*Ian Cooling Collection*)

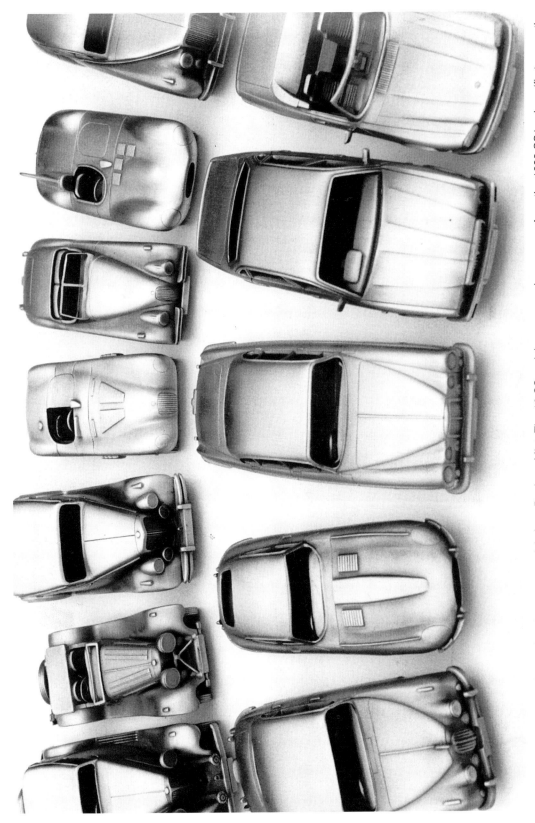

An impressive grouping of 1:43rd scale pewter models from Danbury Mint. The 12 SS and Jaguar cars shown range from the 1933 SS1 saloon (first car on the back row) to the 1988 XJS drophead coupe (last car on the front row). The patina of the metal makes these models especially effective as display items. (*Michael Tate Collection*)

A group of Jaguar car club badges. (*Ian Cooling Collection*)

as a paperweight. This had been lying in a cupboard at a Jaguar agent for many years. This same garage also insisted on giving me a huge chrome-plated mascot, around 8ft long, and the only way I could transport it home was to open the sunroof and drive along with its head sticking out! Like many agents, this one had discarded many unique items, for example an enamel SS wall sign had been used to mix cement on, and consequently was beyond repair.

I have never been able to discover just how many promotional pieces were produced by SS and Jaguar. However, during 1993 some of the personal collection of the company's former deputy chairman, Arthur Whittaker, were sold at auction. These items gave some idea as to the sort of quality mementoes the company made available, probably to distributors and valued customers. Amongst them were inkwells, desk calendars, cigarette boxes, lighters, ashtrays, desk blotters and pen stands, some of them in silver, and most with an SS or Jaguar logo.

Do you remember those toy Jaguars, the ones you had yourself, or those you bought for your children? Then like me you will probably be amazed to discover how many of them were produced. I cannot hope to mention every make available, but here are some of the most popular that I remember:

My first toy Jaguar was an early Dinky Toy model of an SS100. It was rather crude, perhaps, but I loved it and remember being quite upset when someone accidentally trod on it. The little Lesney Matchbox cars were popular during the Fifties. I think they cost about two shillings, perhaps less, and amongst the first were XK120 fixed-heads. Later on I think they made a 3.4 saloon, but I know that the little 120s, complete with box, are now fetching quite high prices.

Dinky Toy cars were made in huge numbers, but few survived in good condition. There was always a good range of Jaguars, including the XK120, several E-types, a Mk X, a 3.4

Less than a tenth of one man's collection of Jaguar models! Keen-eyed fellow collectors will spot such rarities as the Distler XK 120 coupe on the bottom shelf, the group of 1:43rd scale racing car models created by master-craftsman Tim Dyke (middle shelf left) and John Haynes' beautiful 1:24th scale rendition of the 1955 Le Mans-winning D-type on the top shelf. (*Michael Tate Collection*)

Mk II, an XJ6 and even a D-type.

Corgi made some excellent Jaguar toys, beginning with a 2.4 saloon. They also produced a Mk X, an E-type and an XJ6, while the XJS appeared in many guises, including the Saint's car, a police car and a powerboat car. There have also been some very attractive boxed sets.

Spot-on also made Jaguar models, one of the rarest being the XK SS, one of which I saw on display prior to an auction with a price estimation of over £300. The message here is simple: immaculate, boxed toys are the only ones to command high prices. However, if you are like me, the more reasonably priced ones, the sort you buy at jumbles, make ideal decorations for the office, home or garage.

But my favourite collectable items are badges and mascots, which are attractive and easy to store. A few years ago I set out to collect every postwar Jaguar grille badge, and I decided to look for original badges where possible – badges that had seen some use on a car. But what I had overlooked was the fact that most Jaguar badges were made from poor-quality material which does not weather well and cannot be restored.

The first postwar badges are attractive winged items with the Jaguar name and engine size on separate enamel inserts. These are coloured mauve for the 1½-litre, cream for the 2½-litre and black for the 3½-litre. The wings are made from mazak and cannot be replated successfully. A kindly plater pointed this out to me, showing me the mess he had made of a mazak item in the past. Since then, anything in this material that needed replating I have left well alone. I have been fortunate enough to find a set of all three badges in excellent condition, good ones being very scarce. Incidentally, these same badges were used until 1951 on the 2½-litre and 3½-litre Mk Vs.

One of the most attractive badges is the one from the Mk VII; although made from a mazak-type material, these combined mascot badges do not seem to corrode as rapidly as some of their counterparts. But unfortunately, the only suitable place to display one of these badges is on the bonnet of a Mk VII, yet strangely, they have been commanding surprisingly high prices.

Amongst the most sought after badges is that from the XK120, although it was also used on the C-type, and there must have been thousands of them produced. Some – but not all – of the original badges have a maker's name on the back, and for a number of years such badges have been reproduced for the benefit of restorers and it has become impossible to distinguish an original from a suitably aged repro.

The last of the metal badges was to be found on the XK140, although a poor quality mazak winged badge, introduced for the Mk VIII, was in use until the late Sixties on 420s and 420Gs. An XK140 badge has been the only Jaguar one I have been able to have restored properly, *ie* enamelled and replated; original XK140 badges are now very scarce, especially the boot badge.

The first plastic badge appeared on the Mk I 2.4, and since then all Jaguar badges, apart from a couple of exceptions, have been in this material. When new, the badges look magnificent, but sadly they soon deteriorate to the extent that they become unreadable. The manufacturing process must have involved impregnating the colours during the moulding stage, but after a time the colours just faded away. I know of several people who have tried to restore such badges by repainting them from the inside, but without success.

My collection includes plastic badges that are either unused original Jaguar parts or good-quality reproductions. I can see no difference between them, so in the circumstances I have no objection to non-original items. I have some 26 Jaguar grille badges in my display and they look magnificent, the newest being from the XJ40 and the XJS. More ambitious collectors could always try to compete with one very experienced badge collector known to me who has an example of nearly every postwar Jaguar badge produced, be it for the front, side, bootlid or interior. At the last count he had almost 300 different items.

There have been many reports of rare or prototype Jaguar mascots, but I am convinced that there were only four basic official designs, each of which had one or two variations. Introduced in 1938, the first official Jaguar mascot was advertised for sale at two guineas. Designed by the famous motoring artist F Gordon Crosby, these earlier mascots are instantly identifiable by the more finely detailed back legs, triangular or pear-shaped baseplate and one fixing stud. I believe most were made by the factory and bear no markings, but several are supposed to have been made by or on behalf of the designer and these are engraved on the baseplate. I have never seen one of these 'designer' versions, but I understand that in every case the engraving was carried out at a later date. However, Ian Cooling has seen similar additions, in the same style of script, on mascots which are undoubtedly copies/fakes.

These early mascots also vary in both quality and weight, while some I have looked at were very badly pitted beneath the plating. Again this is not an item which should be replated because the alloy could dissolve during the process. The danger, of course, is in stripping off the old chrome. I took one of my early mascots for replating after I had stripped off all the old and peeling chrome by hand. It was a tedious task, and I would not like to have to repeat it, but the effort was more than worth it for the end result – a nicely finished mascot with only a couple of slight pit marks.

No-one seems to be quite sure what these early items were made of, but I have two of

Jaguar produce a number of very tasteful accessories carrying the company logo, all being collector's items of the future, but rather costly. The glossy colour catalogue *The Jaguar Collection* is readily available from main agents, and is itself an interesting piece of Jaguar automobilia.

From the earliest days, Jaguar cars were supplied with a most comprehensive toolkit, but most buyers of secondhand models would be lucky to find one with the kit still intact. The later cars, those with removable kits, such as the compact saloons and the E-types, often lost the entire kit early in their life. Consequently, Jaguar tools – not just complete kits, but individual items from them – have also earned collectable status.

Avid collectors can spend hours discussing the type or colour of felt used in a particular fitted toolbox, or how many different kinds of pliers or screwdrivers may be encountered. Collecting Jaguar tools is quite a science because very few of the items were marked, but enthusiasts seem to have ways of recognizing them, often from quite long distances!

Recently, I saw a stirrup-type foot pump, which was dirty but complete and in good order, being sold at an autojumble for just 50p; the delighted buyer had recognized it as being from an early postwar Jaguar kit. Owners of *concours* cars now have to compete with collectors of certain tools, and quite recently I heard of an unused E-type tool roll changing hands three times during a weekend.

It would take a complete book to describe every item of Jaguar automobilia. Anything and everything Jaguar-related, in seems, is of interest to a collector somewhere, and surely no other make of car in the world has created such an army of avid collectors. My search for badges has led to me meeting collectors of headlamps, race programmes, club magazines, dashboard instruments, posters, hubcaps, company material, radiator grilles and many other items. Some of these collectors, like myself, are Jaguar car enthusiasts while others just have an interest in the automobilia. But all of us have something in common – an appreciation of good design and the pleasure of knowing that maybe some day something new and unexpected will turn up. Well, there's no charge for hoping!

A presentation tray. Interesting features are the two cast bronze Jaguar handles and the very effective Roy Nockolds painting of a Mk II in a landscape setting. (*Ian Cooling Collection*)

The author

MARTIN CROSS was born in Cheshire, but spent his early years in London before returning north in time to begin his secondary education.

A car enthusiast from an early age, he put his first Jaguar – a 1½-litre model – on the road within days of passing his driving test as a 17-year-old. He then became absorbed in a hobby of Jaguar restoration while building a career in the textile industry, and subsequently running his own business specializing in metal treatments.

Recently he became interested in politics and stood as a Liberal Democrat candidate in the 1997 General Election. He names his other major interests as writing, the countryside, most types of music and, when he is not too busy, just relaxing in the garden. He is also an avid collector of British military swords, car radiator badges, and records from the 1950s and 1960s.